dean woods

MANUAL
OF CYCLING

Author Dean Woods in the 1992 World Professional Points Race Championship at Valencia, Spain.

everything you need to know about racing

the dean woods

manual OF CYCLING

Dean Woods

with Rupert Guinness

HarperSports

An imprint of HarperCollinsPublishers

Harper*Sports*
An imprint of HarperCollins*Publishers*, Australia

First published in Australia in 1995

25 Ryde Road, Pymble, Sydney NSW 2073, Australia
31 View Road, Glenfield, Auckland 10, New Zealand
77–85 Fulham Palace Road, London W6 8JB, United Kingdom
Hazelton Lanes, 55 Avenue Road, Suite 2900, Toronto, Ontario M5R 3L2
and 1995 Markham Road, Scarborough, Ontario M1B 5M8, Canada
10 East 53rd Street, New York NY 10032, USA

National Library of Australia Cataloguing-in-Publication data:
    Woods, Dean, 1966- .
    The Dean Woods manual of cycling.
    Bibliography.
    Includes index.

    ISBN 0 207 177805.
        1.Cycling – Training – Handbooks, manuals, etc. 2.Cycling –
        Handbooks, manuals, etc. I.Guinness, Rupert. II.Title.
        III.Title: Manual of cycling
    796.62

Front and back cover photographs by Graham Watson
Illustrations by Ingrid Kwong
Design by Neil Carlyle
Printed in Hong Kong

9 8 7 6 5 4 3 2 1
97 96 95 98

I dedicate this book to my loving wife, Meagan,
who has stood by me through the good times and especially the bad.
Also, to David, for his belief in my abilities.

This book would not have been possible without the following people:
Charlie Walsh
Ian Jarman
Cherub W

We are grateful to the Australian Cycling Federation
for the help they have given us.
Thanks also to the Bicycle Institute of New South Wales
for the use of their photographs.

Three of Australia's leading track stars
fill the podium of the 1994 Commonwealth Games 40-kilometre Points Race:
(left to right) South Australia's Stuart O'Grady and Brett Aitken and Victoria's Dean Woods.

Contents

Dean Woods at the 1990 World Championships in Japan, attempting to better his silver medal win in the 1989 Individual Pursuit.

Fore**word**

Images of the green and gold flashing first over the line in the 1984 Olympics are still vivid in my memory as the almost unbelievable happening. In the Australian quartet of the team pursuit was a youngster who had already left his mark on world cycling, having notched up a World Championship and at 17 putting an Olympic gold under his belt. It must have been a proud moment for him and now it is with pride on my part that I write this foreword to Dean's book.

I will start by saying that in all sports there are very few athletes who come into the category of being what is termed 'very coachable' — that is, a coach's dream. It has been my pleasure that I have had this opportunity to work with Dean and to experience with him the heights he has attained in his sport — gold, silver and bronze Olympic medals and two world medals to show for all the years of training and years of sacrifice. Many a sportsperson would never dream of achieving so much.

Along the way with the medals and glory there have also been disappointments. Dean, to his great credit, has taken all the knocks on the chin, usually smiling bravely at the same time — stuff which shows what a truly great sportsperson is made of!

In the history of sport, great athletes are often only given recognition by the media well after their retirement, a famous cyclist once being referred to as a 'great old man of cycling'. As one of Australia's great present-day sports heroes, should we begin calling Dean (well before his retirement) a 'great old man'? Young cyclists just beginning to make their mark on the stage of world cycling probably think of him in this way already. But at the ripe old age of 29 he's still giving them a good run for their money.

To Dean, I say thank you for your invitation to write this foreword, congratulations on your achievements and the best of luck with your future career.

Charlie Walsh
OLYMPIC TRACK CYCLING COACH
HEAD COACH,
AUSTRALIAN INSTITUTE OF SPORT,
TRACK CYCLING

The peloton begins its daily voyage in the 1993 Tour de France.

Intro**duction**

It was on 7 November 1869 in France that the first ever point-to-point bicycle race was organised. Paris–Rouen was won by an Englishman named James Moore.

The event not only signalled the transition of the bicycle as a means of transport to the arena of sporting competition, it also marked the birth of a sport which would — more than a century later — touch deeply into the four corners of the world on both road and track.

Bicycle racing's roots are still fixed firmly in European soil where its genesis was as a working-class outlet of physical endeavour. This is hardly surprising, since the *first* racers — many of them from an impoverished rural background — used competition as a means of earning money to buy dinner for their families.

Today in Australia, New Zealand, the United States, South America and South East Asia cycling is becoming more and more popular as a sport. And while the working-class image still holds firm in the 'old world', cycling's image in these new frontiers encompasses all social classes.

Not every cycling fan may aspire to join élite events like the annual Tour de France, but the increasing number of people seen pedalling throughout inner-city, residential and country regions is testimony to cycle sport's growth.

Cycling is *not* just about road and track. The last decade has seen the rapid evolution of mountain biking from a gimmick to a fully recognised Olympic sport. The sister sports of triathlon and duathlon have played their parts too, thanks to the presence of cycling in their agendas. And one can't ignore the recreational pleasures of a sport where sea is its only real barrier!

Increased interest in cycling means spin-off returns for the sport, including an upturn in retail manufacturing, expanding media interest, a boost in governmental support and funding for Olympic and national squads, bigger investment in training and racing facilities and — most importantly — better education in how to maximise personal performance.

And it is with this last point in mind that *The Dean Woods Manual of Cycling* has been written. This book is aimed at anyone caught up by the cycling phenomenon — from the enthusiast and beginner to the élite amateur.

Every aspect of cycle sport is covered in this 'bible', from the basics of getting started to the finer points of competition.

We look at the varying demands and necessities behind road, track and mountain-bike racing. There is also a thorough assessment of training principles based on the gold-medal winning theories of the Australian Cycling Federation — physiological and psychological preparation, the requirements of a sound diet, massage and first aid. There are chapters on the dos and don'ts of basic bicycle maintenance and an examination of the history behind the great events and riders of a sport so steeped in tradition.

The Dean Woods Manual of Cycling can't guarantee you the wins you want but, studied and followed closely, we feel you'll go a long way to maximising your potential.

Dean Woods and *Rupert Guinness*

Author Dean Woods climbing one of the many tortuous ascents in the 1990 Tour of Spain.

xi

1 Road **Cycling**

Road cycling is now one of our most popular forms of leisure and exercise. Bicycles are still frequently used as transport — especially within inner-city limits where traffic restrictions which slow down cars and buses are no problem to the cyclist. The fact that cycling has evolved into one of our fastest-growing hobbies as well is a measure of society's growing awareness of the importance of health and fitness.

However, for the millions of people who take to the roads around the world, cycling offers much more than just improved physical condition. For those with a competitive edge, racing can fulfil an ambitious streak. And for the adventurous, cycling is a terrific way of touring in which, either as an individual or in a group, you can discover and take in the sights at any pace you like.

As this opening chapter explains, there's more to road cycling than getting on a bike and pedalling. It's a sport without limits, but one that still needs special planning and preparation in order to reap the full benefits from it.

Choosing the **Right** Bike

Before buying the ideal bicycle there are two things to decide: firstly, you must choose what type of cycling activity you are going to do and secondly, you need to calculate the amount of money you are willing to spend.

Every cyclist dreams of buying the ultimate custom-designed bicycle, made up of a personally built frame and specially chosen gears, componentry and wheels. Each year research in wind tunnels has seen bicycle frame and component design change to be more aerodynamic, or less wind resistant, and therefore to offer greater speed potential. Not all designs suit all riders; often the most advanced research is made with one élite rider, such as Greg LeMond or Miguel Induraín, being used as a test model.

However, it was in the 1980 Olympic Games at Moscow, when Switzerland's Robert Dill-Bundi won the individual pursuit title using a low-profile bicycle for the first time in world-class competition, that the diversity of bicycle design took a major step. Since then not a season has passed without some radical design appearing in the pursuit of aerodynamic speed.

If you're a beginner, though, start with a standard road bicycle. Emulating Dill-Bundi and the horde of pioneering greats in design can wait till later when you are at a better level. For now, don't be hesitant about buying a pre-built or set-up bicycle 'off the rack'.

Second-hand bicycles are also good for beginners. You can buy these from shops or through local clubs. Proficient riders often use them as their second bicycle for training. When you're buying one for the first time, just make sure that you have been measured up correctly so that you get the right size.

There's no point in spending A$2000 on a bicycle if you are only going to ride on weekends. You need to work out how often you will use your bicycle, how many kilometres you will ride and also if you are going to cycle for leisure, touring or racing.

Whatever you choose, if you are a beginner, it is probably best to buy the least expensive equipment and focus on gaining confidence and experience with your bike. You can use this time to decide on what direction you will take in the sport. If you do finally decide to race, a beginner shouldn't need to spend more than A$1000 for their first proper racing bicycle.

As for finding the best location to buy a bicycle, shop around. Word of mouth is a good way of finding a reliable cycle shop. Make a list of the shops in your area and find out where other cyclists go to buy their equipment. A good place should willingly give free and friendly advice to potential customers. Avoid those shops in which the proprietors are sales-driven and grudging with their time.

By the time you have located your most suitable shop you will also have developed a good sense of what equipment and products are available. The question of what to get and what not to get is quite complex when buying a road bicycle. These are the points worth remembering when choosing one.

Sizing-up

When you begin choosing your bicycle, you need to know what measurements you have for body weight, height and inner-leg length.

If you can, you should go into the shop prepared with specific sizing-up figures. If you don't have these, one of the prerequisites of any good shop is that they will size you up properly before selling you a bicycle.

Most major bicycle shops have an indoor 'measuring bike' which can change its dimensions according to your bodily proportions while you sit on it. With this, the head stem, the seat post and the length of the top tube can be adjusted. This will accurately measure what size your bike's dimensions should be.

Another positioning device is the Fit Kit, a portable American-made machine which is available in Australia at some specialist bicycle shops. It comes with computer software on which you record arm, inside-leg, thigh, foot and upper-torso lengths. When fed into a computer, the programme will tell you your required frame size, head-stem length and seat height.

■ Custom-made Bicycles

If you're having your bicycle custom-made, one of the benefits of an adjustable measuring bike is that you and the builder can see together what you need before any work is started. (There is nothing more frustrating than parting with your cash after having waited for months in anticipation while your bike frame was being built, only to discover the frame size you end up with is totally wrong!)

However, if this machine is not available, then sizing-up can still be done by an expert mechanic or frame builder. If you know very little about bicycles it is best to ask the bicycle shop or your club about sizing-up. Don't ask just one person, though — ask several people for their opinions. Then assess the various options and see how they work in with the shop's assessment.

FRAME SIZE

The Sizing Chart

Inseam		Frame size		Seat height*	
inches	cm	inches	cm	inches	cm
26	66.0	16.9	42.9	23.0	58.3
26.5	67.3	17.2	43.8	23.4	59.4
27	68.6	17.6	44.6	23.8	60.6
27.5	69.9	17.9	45.4	24.3	61.7
28	71.1	18.2	46.2	24.7	62.8
28.5	72.4	18.5	47.1	25.2	63.9
29	73.7	18.9	47.9	25.6	65.0
29.5	74.9	19.2	48.7	26.0	66.2
30	76.2	19.5	49.5	26.5	67.3
30.5	77.5	19.8	50.4	26.9	68.4
31	78.7	20.2	51.2	27.4	69.5
31.5	80.0	20.5	52.0	27.8	70.6
32	81.3	20.8	52.8	28.3	71.8
32.5	82.6	21.1	53.7	28.7	72.9
33	83.8	21.5	54.5	29.1	74.0
33.5	85.1	21.8	55.3	29.6	75.1
34	86.4	22.1	56.1	30.0	76.3
34.5	87.6	22.4	57.8	30.5	77.4
35	88.9	22.8	57.8	30.9	78.5
35.5	90.2	23.1	58.6	31.3	79.6
36	91.4	23.4	59.4	31.8	80.7
36.5	92.7	23.7	60.3	32.2	81.9
37	94.0	24.1	61.1	32.7	83.0
37.5	95.3	24.4	61.9	33.1	84.1
38	96.5	24.7	62.7	33.6	85.2
38.5	97.8	25	63.6	34	86.3
39	99.1	25.4	64.4	34.4	87.5
39.5	100.3	25.7	65.2	34.9	88.6
40	101.6	26.0	66.0	35.3	89.7
40.5	102.9	26.3	66.9	35.8	90.8
41	104.1	26.7	67.7	36.2	92.0
41.5	105.4	27.0	68.5	36.6	93.1
42	106.7	27.3	69.3	37.1	94.2
42.5	108.0	27.6	70.2	37.5	95.3
43	109.2	28.0	71.0	38.0	96.4
43.5	110.5	28.3	71.8	38.4	97.6

*Distance from top of the saddle to the centre of the bottom-bracket axle

Two Australian professionals use two standards of bicycle design and construction.
THIS PAGE: Scott Sunderland rides a conventional Zullo made of Columbus tubing;
NEXT PAGE: Neil Stephens rides a highly advanced (and expensive) carbon-fibre monocoque
frame by Look.

FRAME
SIZES •••

Metric Conversion Chart

inches	cm	inches	cm	inches	cm
17	43.2	21.5	54.6	26	66.0
17.5	44.5	22	55.9	26.5	67.3
18	45.7	22.5	57.2	27	68.6
18.5	47.0	23	58.4	27.5	69.9
19	48.3	23.5	59.7	28	71.1
19.5	49.5	24	61.0	28.5	72.4
20	50.8	24.5	62.2	29	73.7
20.5	52.1	25	63.5		
21	53.3	25.5	64.8		

FRAME
GEOMETRY

Variations on Frame Geometry

When we refer to a frame by the angle of its seat tube and head tube, we assume an average frame size of 58 centimetres (or 23 inches). But there are many different frame sizes, obviously, and geometry varies with frame size.

Frame size	Seat-tube angle	Head-tube angle
47 cm and less	74 degrees	72.5 degrees
47.5 cm–52 cm	73 degrees	73 degrees
52.5 cm–61 cm	72 degrees	74 degrees
61 cm and greater	71.5 degrees	74.5 degrees

(This chart gives only a rough indication of the variation in frame geometry. Every manufacturer has a different range of seat and head-tube angles for its bikes.)

•••

Nearly all frame builders measure their bicycles from centre to centre (centre of the bottom bracket to the centre of the seat lug) on all measurements. However, make it a habit to refer to your measurements as 'centre-to-centre', as some builders refer to centre-to-top (to top of the seat lug). The main reason why centre-to-centre measurements are more accurate is because varying sizes of lugs, or brazed joints to the tubing, can alter centre-to-top measurements.

Follow these steps when using a Fit Kit-style adjustable frame bike.

1. Seat–tube length

- Adjust the saddle forwards or backwards so the middle of the seat is centred over the seat post.
- Now adjust the seat post so that it is extended approximately 10 to 15 centimetres (4 to 6 inches) out of the frame.
- Place one pedal at its furthest point from the seat (at the '5-o'clock' position).
- Now, to determine the correct length of the seat tube, mount the bicycle wearing your cycling shoes and place your heel over the centre of the pedal axle (which should still be in the 5-o'clock position). The saddle should be high enough so that your leg is slightly bent at the knee. The seat tube of the measuring bike can be adjusted until this position is reached.

2. Top–tube length

- Set the head-stem length (that is, the horizontal distance) to between 12 and 13 centimetres (4³/₄ and 5 inches). This has been found to be the best length for strength and handling. Remember to try out the same make of handlebars as you'll be using on your custom-made bike.
- Put both feet in the pedals wearing your cycling shoes, and position your right foot in line with the down tube. Get into a racing position by placing your hands on the drops, or lower section of the handlebars.
- Now adjust the length of the top tube to the ideal position — i.e. have the inside of your elbow lined up with the centre of the outside of your knee. This position once set can be slightly lengthened or shortened, depending on how comfortable you feel. Ask someone else to check your position too, to make sure that your back is straight, and not arched. When you reach the ideal position, you'll have the correct length of the top tube.

8

SEAT-TUBE LENGTH • **TOP-TUBE LENGTH** • • • • • • • • • • • • • • • • • • •

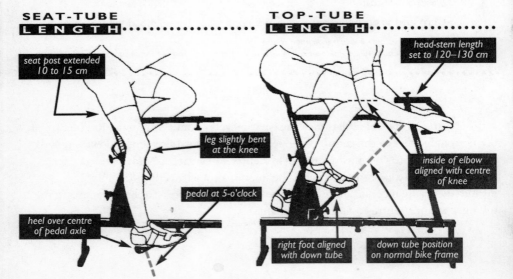

seat post extended 10 to 15 cm

head-stem length set to 120–130 cm

leg slightly bent at the knee

inside of elbow aligned with centre of knee

pedal at 5-o'clock

heel over centre of pedal axle

right foot aligned with down tube

down tube position on normal bike frame

3. Head–stem height

This will depend on how tall you are and the size of your bicycle frame. Getting the measurement right will improve aerodynamics and comfort. A good guideline is for the top of your head stem to be 5 to 8 centimetres (2 to 3 inches) lower than the top of your seat.

◼ Second-hand and Off-the-rack Bicycles

Sizing-up for a second-hand or pre-made bicycle is a simple procedure because three things are already determined: the top tube, seat tube and seat angle of the bicycle.

To position your seat correctly, the first step is to find out the ideal measurement from the tip of the saddle to the middle of the bottom bracket. This is determined by mounting the bicycle and placing the pedals in a horizontal, quarter-to-3 position. A vertical line should pass from the tip of the knee to the centre of the pedal while you are in race position (*see illustration on following page*). The seat will need to be adjusted backwards or forwards until this vertical line is established. When you have achieved this line, simply hang a plumb bob from the tip of the seat and measure the horizontal distance from the line to the middle of the bottom bracket.

To find your correct seat height, mount the bicycle, wearing your cycling shoes, and adjust the seat height up or down so that your leg is slightly bent while the pedal is at the 5-o'clock position and your heel is on the centre of the pedal axle.

For your head-stem length, get into the racing position with your pedals in line with the down tube once more. See how cramped up or stretched out you are. Try to get into a position so that the line of your forearm is parallel to your thigh. Make sure that your final position is comfortable at the three points of contact with the handlebars — the brake-lever covers, the top of the bars and the drops.

As you will not be able to alter the size of the frame, you will need to compensate for this by buying a head stem of a different length. If you are fortunate enough to know someone who owns a wide selection, ask if you can experiment with different lengths before buying one. If you can't do this, perhaps the bike shop owner will let you sample a few second-hand sizes if there are any available. Once you buy a new head stem it can't be exchanged if you should make the wrong choice.

Don't forget, though, that whatever anyone says, in the end it is how you feel on the bike that is important. It will take a lot of trial and error to find the most ideal position, especially if you are new to the sport. Take heart from the fact that even the top professionals are known to change their position from year to year. In some cases, they do it from month to month!

Positioning

The size of your bicycle frame and your position on it are extremely important. These factors affect comfort and riding efficiency, and a properly sized bicycle and position can avert serious muscle and tendon injury.

The basic principle of bicycle positioning is more or less the same whether you are riding a standard bicycle on the road, on the track or competing in a time trial. The idea is to have your body weight evenly distributed over both wheels. Across the various disciplines, though, measurements and position will still vary slightly depending on personal preferences and the environment you are riding in.

For example, in road racing as a general rule your seat should be slightly more behind the centre bracket than for track racing or time trials. However, when you are actually on the road you confront different terrain all the time. When you come to a flat section you will naturally pull yourself over the centre bracket more. And when going uphill there is a tendency to ride further behind the bracket.

Once you have the right sized frame and have set the seat and stem positions, you may need to make further minor adjustments.

10

Anatomy

Frames

When choosing your frame, think about the material it is built of. These days frames are made from a variety of materials — steel, carbon-fibre, aluminium and titanium, the latter two becoming increasingly popular. They all have their pluses and minuses, with the top of the range in each material generally being very well built.

Whatever the material, the price of frames hinges on the manufacturing costs involved. Steel frames are generally cheaper because they cost less to build, whereas aluminium (although a cheap raw material) is dearer because aluminium frames require more expensive manufacturing methods. The same goes for carbon-fibre frames which are generally made from specially built moulds. With titanium, the costs are even more because costly construction methods are used to build a frame and the material itself is expensive (it is, however, very long-lasting).

If you do a lot of racing, you may not want carbon-fibre or aluminium frames because the spring in the forks disappears after about 12 months due to constant stress. These frames also tend not to be stiff enough, and those which are come at a very high price. This is fine if you're riding for a team which provides new frames all the time. But for the average person it's not necessary.

The type of frame you buy is really only an issue when you are a top-level rider racing in specific events. As a beginner, it's best to start with a steel frame because they are cheaper and more durable. Within this category there are several good tubing sets: Reynolds of England, Columbus of Italy and Ichiwata and Tange from Japan (two brands which have come a long way in recent years). These and other brands are available in countries throughout the world. Most top frame builders in your area will use them, but imported frames are not necessarily of better quality.

Reynolds can be recommended. They make good 753-millimetre and 653-millimetre steel tubing. (753 and 653 are measurements for the density of the tubing.) Some frames are thicker at the joints, or lugs, to absorb stress, and thin in the tubes. The 753, for example, is very light and strong.

Remember that a second-hand frame can look brand-new with a new paint job. Just check two things: one, that it is not cracked and two, that it is not too old. Check also that it hasn't been damaged in a crash. It's fairly easy to tell if second-hand equipment is in good condition or not. Look for scratches, marks and any strange bends or dents. You can apply these rules to many pieces of equipment, although gears, centre brackets and head sets should be new even in a second-hand bicycle. This is because they will not last the lifetime of the frame. With wheels and hubs, always check they roll evenly, or 'true'.

It is rare that a shop or person will deliberately try to sell damaged equipment — word would get around too quickly. But don't be complacent. Rip-offs can sometimes occur. So if you have doubts or concerns about a product someone is trying to sell you, don't be afraid to ask someone else what they think. You could even visit the shop again with a friend or fellow rider who may be more knowledgeable than you.

Wheels

The choice of wheels depends on what event or circumstances you are cycling in. If you decide to get customised wheels, make sure that the person who makes them up is an experienced wheel builder. If you are thinking of buying a second-hand pair it's easy to tell if they have had a lot of heavy use. Look at the side of the rims to see the extent of wear marks from the brakes. Or open up the axle and see what condition the grease is in: if it's really dirty and full of sand and grit you'll know that the wheels are either old or have been ridden in harsh and wet conditions.

8-speed rear cluster

An increasing number of road bikes are being fitted with aerodynamic wheels for road racing, whereas previously their appearance was restricted to time trial events. Dual brake/gear levers are now standard on nearly all quality road bikes.

There is a variety of aerodynamic wheel designs for time-trialling: disc wheels, three and four-bladed wheels and those with large and small V-sectioned rims. First we will look at the requirements of a normal bicycle wheel.

dual brake/gear levers

drop handlebars

deep section aero rims

high-pressure tyres

double front chain-rings

clipless pedals

A: French Mavic 3G composite carbon-fibre three-spoked wheel with interchangeable hub cartridges for front or rear application.

B: American Zipp 440 carbon-fibre deep-rimmed spoked front wheel.

C: Italian 32-spoked Campagnolo Omega aero rim.

D: American Zipp Disc carbon-fibre rear wheel.

E: French Roval lightweight 18-spoked wheel.

F: Australian Aerovantage heat-shrunk mylar-covered wheel. An inexpensive alternative to increased aerodynamic efficiency by using your existing rear wheel.

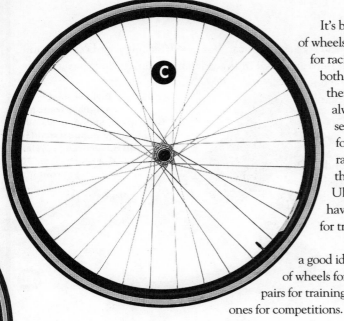

It's best to have at least two sets of wheels: one for training and one for racing. If you used one set for both purposes you'd soon wear them out. Or you'd find yourself always rushing to get the one set you have in top condition for racing. By saving a set for racing alone, it will always be there and ready for use.

Ultimately, it would be ideal to have three sets of wheels — one for training and two for racing.

For élite competitors it's a good idea to have at least two pairs of wheels for racing and another two pairs for training, saving the most expensive ones for competitions.

■ Rims

The key element to a wheel, most good rims are made of heat-treated aluminium by a process of anodising which gives them a black colour. Weights vary for all rims, with the lighter grades usually being used for track racing or time trials. It's better in road races to go for a heavier, sturdier type.

The best rims are Mavic GP4s for general use on both road and track. They are a middle-of-the-range brand, but provide the top quality of more expensive marks like Campagnolo.

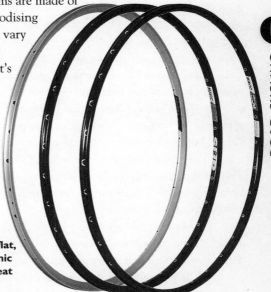

Left to right: French Mavic SUP (made using a machine-welded process which produces a flat, seamless rim); French Mavic open SUP ceramic (the ceramic-coated brake surface reduces heat build-up and improves wet-weather braking); Australian Velocity Aero alloy rim.

■ Hubs

All you need now are hubs and spokes. Hubs can be made from alloy, carbon-fibre and even titanium, though most hubs are alloy. In this domain Campagnolo is regarded as both the most stylish and the best. It's worth paying more for this brand: unlike poor-quality, cheaper hub brands whose bearings can wear out quickly, Campagnolo hubs wear in and improve as they get older. Today sealed bearings are also used more than the old loose-bearing style purely because they need less maintenance.

**A: US Zipp Ballistic lightweight carbon-fibre front hub;
B: Japanese Shimano 105 alloy front hub (a popular standard on middle-range cycles);
C: French Mavic 501 front hub.**

■ Spokes

The choice for quality spokes is more limited. Spokes are normally made from stainless steel, although it is becoming more common for élite cyclists to use carbon-fibre spokes which — while more expensive — are lighter while still providing strength. The most reputable international brand is DT from Switzerland. It is estimated that 95% of top professional teams in Europe use these spokes because of their strength and reliability.

Spokes come in a variety of thicknesses and gauges, but choice depends on the number of spokes you need and your weight and cycling style. Spokes also come in two designs — the conventional round style and the flat or bladed sort which is more aerodynamic. Wheels with fewer spokes provide more aerodynamism but less strength. Wheel builders attempt to compensate for this by using various lacing patterns.

For general racing and training, traditional spoked wheels are the most common. They come in a range of 24 to 40 spokes, with 32 to 36 being the most frequently used because a greater number provides more reliability and strength (if one spoke breaks you can continue riding).

Wheels with fewer spokes (24 or 28) bear less structural strength. But they are good for time trials where smoother surface conditions mean there is less possibility of damaging their more fragile make up, or on mountains where less weight is an advantage.

While you might want to go for lighter or more aerodynamic spokes, be aware of two things — your body weight and build, and the terrain you are cycling on. It is best to go for heavier-gauge or thicker spokes if you are a big person or you're cycling on bad roads. Similarly, unless you are light or are riding on smooth roads, it's advisable to buy wheels which have a standard 36-spoke wheel. Riders like four-times Tour de France champion Miguel Induraín can get away with fewer spokes because their style is so smooth, but someone of Induraín's size without his experience would only tear apart a wheel with fewer spokes.

Tyres

There are two standard types of tyre: high-pressures — known as 'clinchers' in the United States — which are detachable from the rim and have a separate inner tube; and singles — called 'tubs' in Great Britain and 'sew-ups' in the US — which have the tube sewn into the tyre and are glued on to the rim.

Make sure that whatever type you use, it is designed for the style of wheel rim you have.

Depending on the country you're in, you may find regulations which determine what kind of tyres you are allowed to use. For example, in Australia racing cyclists under 17 years of age are not allowed to use singles, although in Europe racing cyclists of all ages can use them in track and road competitions.

The choice of tyre is enormous. Price is a major factor. You can pay from A$10 to A$350 for a single, so be realistic with your needs. Whatever you buy, save your best tyres for racing and the cheaper ones for training and small, less important races. High-pressure tyres, being cheaper, are better saved for training, although some professional teams in Europe have been using prototype models in competition recently.

In good weather, high-pressure tyres are great. But many riders have complained that in the wet they are, contrary to popular belief, more vulnerable to punctures than singles. This is because loose gravel, broken glass or even fallen twigs are less easily seen in wet conditions. And while these objects can pierce singles as well when passed over, they are more likely to cause the thicker and firmer outer tube of a high-pressure tyre to pinch the inner tube and puncture it. (Singles are less likely to puncture because the inner and outer tube are constructed as one

Two examples of high-pressure road-racing tyres: Continental Competition GP single and Continental Grand Prix tubular.

tyre, not in two parts as a high-pressure is.) Worse still, high-pressures have a tendency to hold far less traction on the road than singles. However, manufacturers are constantly trying to develop better products and may come up with the answer to these problems. It is also generally accepted that singles are lighter and more reliable to use in competition.

For a recommended choice, use the Italian Vittoria brand for road racing, for wet or dry conditions. For good high-pressures, use Michelin from France or Continental from Germany.

With your frame, wheels and tyres chosen, you now need the componentry — the brakes and gears — to go with them. This is also an area you should be cautious about because there are many manufacturers and systems available and, as with wheels and frames, there are new developments in these products every year.

Brakes

Don't go for the cheapest brand and model, but also be wary of choosing the most expensive just because you've seen the top professionals use them. Professional teams are paid to use the latest, top-of-the-range products. After all, they are the manufacturer's shop window. If you buy this type of componentry you might not know exactly how to set it up and you may end up spending even more money getting a bicycle shop mechanic to correct your mistakes than you bargained for. An alignment only needs to be slightly 'out' and the whole brake or gear system can be out too. (On the big pro teams, riders simply hand their bikes to their salaried team mechanic whenever there is a problem.)

Years ago, the Italian manufacturer Campagnolo was regarded as the top-of-the-range manufacturer for their brakes and gears. Since then, Japanese companies have invested in research and, after several years of development, their products are considered to be up to par with Campagnolo. Two Japanese firms in particular who have come a long way in recent years are Shimano and Suntour. They match their rivals in being expensive, but at least they've given cyclists more choice. Now brake choice depends more on personal taste. Several can be recommended: from the top-of-the-range level — Campagnolo C Record and Shimano Dura-Ace — to a good, mid-priced quality model — Shimano 600.

When choosing your brake cables make sure they are positioned within the handlebars and not protruding out above them, as was the case up until the last decade. It will improve aerodynamism and also give your bike a cleaner and slicker look.

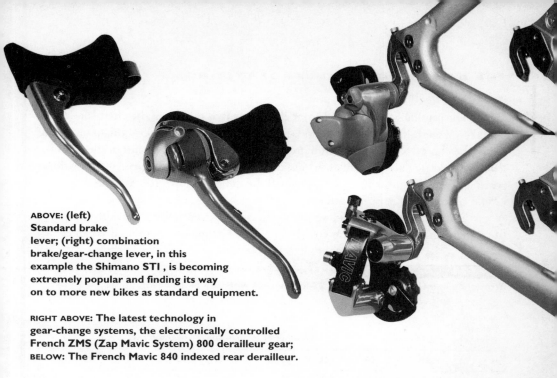

ABOVE: (left)
Standard brake
lever; (right) combination
brake/gear-change lever, in this
example the Shimano STI , is becoming
extremely popular and finding its way
on to more new bikes as standard equipment.

RIGHT ABOVE: The latest technology in
gear-change systems, the electronically controlled
French ZMS (Zap Mavic System) 800 derailleur gear;
BELOW: The French Mavic 840 indexed rear derailleur.

Gears

Before going into gearing selection, it is important to understand how gears work. Gears are changed by a lever system on the down tube or (as in recent years) on the handlebars adjoining the brake system. Basically, gears provide you with a range of pedal resistances for riding comfortably and efficiently in various terrain.

You will hear people talk about small gears and big gears. These refer to gear ratios and are dependent upon what position a rider has the chain on the rear cluster and front chain-ring (*see gear chart on following page*). The smaller the gear, the easier your pedal resistance will be and vice versa. You would use small gears going uphill and bigger gears going downhill or on flat sections while in a sprint or attack.

If you are a beginner it's best to settle for gearing which is positioned on the down tube and which is not an automated or 'click-shift' system where the gears simply slip into place with a shift of the lever. Why? Because a free or 'ratchet' system where you have to find the gear when you shift will educate you in developing an instinctive feel for the gears. Automated gear systems are something you can buy later when you've got more experience.

Of the many brands, Campagnolo is one of the most expensive systems. Shimano Dura-Ace can be just as expensive; they have a range of three or four group sets which all work well. Suntour is also expensive. (It is good, but it doesn't seem to last as long as the others.)

The purpose of a gear chart is to work out the effectiveness of the gear combination you are using with the rear and front derailleur. This is valued in inches per pedal stroke (to give centimetres, multiply this figure by 2.54).

The gearing you use on the front chain-ring is at the top of the chart (under 'Number of teeth in chain-wheel') and the rear free-wheel (or cog) gearing is along the left of the chart ('Number of teeth in free-wheel sprocket'). The figures in the chart itself are the calculated distances the respective combinations will give you using those gearings. For example, a 52 x 14 gearing will theoretically move 100.3 inches (254.8 centimetres) per pedal stroke.

Using the same example, we can see how the equation works: dividing 52 (the front chain-ring) by 14 (the rear cog) gives 3.714. The number of times this can be

GEAR RATIOS
CHART ··

(distance in inches travelled on a 27-inch wheel with one pedal revolution)

Number of teeth in free-wheel sprocket

Number of teeth in chain-wheel sprocket

	38	39	40	41	42	43	44	45	46
12	85.5	87.8	90	92.2	94.5	96.7	99	101.3	103.5
13	78.9	81	83.1	85.2	87.2	89.3	91.4	93.5	95.5
14	73.3	75.2	77.1	79.1	81	82.9	84.9	86.8	88.7
15	68.4	70.2	72	73.8	75.6	77.4	79.2	81	82.8
16	64.1	65.8	67.5	69.2	70.9	72.6	74.3	75.9	77.6
17	60.4	61.9	63.5	65.1	66.7	68.3	69.9	71.5	73.1
18	57	58.5	60	61.5	63	64.5	66.0	67.5	69
19	54	55.4	56.8	58.3	59.7	61.1	62.5	63.9	65.4
20	51.3	52.7	54	55.4	56.7	58.1	59.4	60.8	62.1
21	48.9	50.1	51.4	52.7	54	55.3	56.6	57.9	59.1
22	46.6	47.9	49.1	50.3	51.5	52.8	54	55.2	56.5
23	44.6	45.8	47	48.1	49.3	50.5	51.7	52.8	54
24	42.8	43.9	45	46.1	47.3	48.4	49.5	50.6	51.8
25	41	42.1	43.2	44.3	45.4	46.4	47.5	48.6	49.7
26	39.5	40.5	41.5	42.6	43.6	44.7	45.7	46.7	47.8
27	38	39	40	41	42	43	44	45	46
28	36.6	37.6	38.6	39.5	40.5	41.5	42.4	43.4	44.4
29	35.4	36.3	37.2	38.2	39.1	40	41	41.9	42.8
30	34.2	35.1	36	36.9	37.8	38.7	39.6	40.5	41.4
31	33.1	34	34.8	35.7	36.6	37.5	39.3	39.2	40.1
32	32.1	32.9	33.8	34.6	35.4	36.3	37.1	38	38.8
33	31.1	31.9	32.7	33.5	34.4	35.2	36	36.8	37.6
34	30.2	31	31.8	32.6	33.4	34.1	34.9	35.7	36.5

divided into 100.3 is 27, so the diameter of the wheel is 27 inches (3.714 × 27 = 100.3).

In most countries there are roll-out restrictions for juniors, both male and female. The roll-out is the distance travelled by one revolution of the bike wheel when the highest gear ratio is selected, i.e. the smallest rear (free-wheel) sprocket and the largest front (chain-wheel) sprocket. In Australia, restrictions are: under 19 years, 7.9 metres (8.6 yards); under 17, 6.5 metres (7.1 yards); under 15, 6.0 metres (6.5 yards); under 13, 5.5 metres (6.0 yards); under 11, 5.5 metres (6.0 yards).

• •

Number of teeth in chain-wheel sprocket

47	48	49	50	51	52	53	54	55	56
105.7	108	110.2	112.5	114.8	117	119.2	121.5	123.7	126
97.6	99.7	101.8	103.8	105.9	108	110.1	112.2	114.2	116.3
90.6	92.6	94.5	96.4	98.4	100.3	102.2	104.1	106.1	108
84.6	86.4	88.2	90	91.8	93.6	95.4	97.2	99	100.8
79.3	81	82.7	84.4	86.1	87.8	89.4	91.1	92.8	94.5
74.6	76.2	77.8	79.4	81	82.6	84.2	85.8	87.4	88.9
70.5	72	73.5	75	76.5	78	79.5	81	82.5	84
66.8	68.2	69.6	71.1	72.5	73.9	75.3	76.7	78.2	79.6
63.5	64.8	66.2	67.5	68.9	70.2	71.6	72.9	74.3	75.6
60.4	61.7	63	64.3	65.6	66.9	68.1	69.4	70.7	72
57.7	58.9	60.1	61.4	62.6	63.8	65	66.3	67.5	68.7
55.2	56.3	57.5	58.7	59.9	61	62.2	63.4	64.6	65.7
52.9	54	55.1	56.3	57.4	58.5	59.6	60.8	61.9	63
50.8	51.8	52.9	54	55.1	56.2	57.2	58.3	59.4	60.5
48.8	49.8	50.9	51.9	53	54	55	56.1	57.1	58.2
47	48	49	50	51	52	53	54	55	56
45.3	46.3	47.3	48.2	49.2	50.1	51.1	52.1	53	54
43.8	44.7	45.6	46.6	47.5	48.4	49.3	50.3	51.2	52.1
42.3	43.2	44.1	45	45.9	46.8	47.7	48.6	49.5	50.4
40.9	41.8	42.7	43.5	44.4	45.3	46.2	47	47.9	48.8
39.7	40.5	41.3	42.2	43	43.9	44.7	45.6	46.4	47.3
38.5	39.3	40.1	40.9	41.7	42.5	43.4	44.2	45	45.8
37.3	38.1	38.9	39.7	40.5	41.3	42.1	42.9	43.7	44.5

ROAD CYCLING

Saddles

The saddle is obviously a vital part of the bicycle. All-leather saddles used to be common. Today, like wooden tennis rackets, they are a thing of the past. Top models here include Rolls, Turbo, Selle Italia, Selle Bassano Vuelta, San Marco Concor, Turbo Matic, Elite, ISCA, Vetta SP and Rigida.

What suits one person may be uncomfortable for another. And men and women have differently shaped pelvic bones. Some saddles are specifically designed for a woman's wider pelvis; others have cushioning and durable gel in them which provides ideal extra comfort for touring or races on cobblestones.

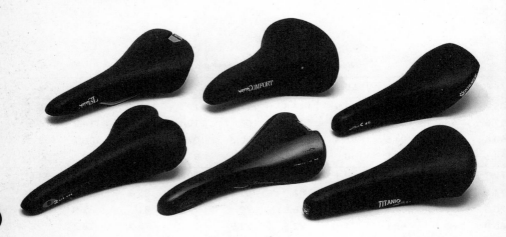

Clockwise: **Vetta SL** (road); **Vetta Comfort** (road); **Bontrager C40** (MTB); **Avocet 02** (road), **Selle Italia** (titanium carbon-fibre) **Flite Evolution** (road); **San Marco Titani 200** (road).

Handlebars

Road-bike handlebars, unlike those on mountain bikes, are rounded so as to be more aerodynamic and to accommodate better positioning for attacking and sprinting.

When choosing handlebars the main thing to check is that they are not too narrow. They should be equivalent to the width of your shoulders. When handlebars are narrow not only can they restrict your breathing but they can also cause back discomfort. Don't go for ones which are too wide, though: handlebars which are bigger than your shoulders could lead to difficulties in handling your bike. And they will create a greater surface area, reducing aerodynamics.

Remember to buy the same brand of handlebars as your head stem as most bars and stems will only fit properly into the same brands. Trying to fit different brands

Everyone loves a winner ... and their bike. Here, aficionados admire Englishman Chris Boardman's Corima after he broke the World Hour Record on it at Bordeaux in July 1993.

together is often difficult, if not impossible, and you also run the risk of the fittings being too loose or becoming damaged.

Handlebars come in various materials. Most are made of aluminium for the road, which is light and durable. Top brands include Cinelli and TTT of Italy. Some handlebars are also made of heat-treated aluminium; Italmanubri of Italy is a leading producer of this type.

Handlebar choice doesn't stop there for the more motivated cyclist. Development is going ahead every year in this area. And there is now a wide variety of models and designs for specific and personal choice. This is especially relevant in time-trialling where handlebar design affects both aerodynamics and performance.

The greatest development in the last decade has been the creation of the triathlete handlebar, or tri-bar, which positions the rider in a skier's crouch. The name comes from the triathlon event where these handlebars were first used. Nowadays they are almost as important as having pedals on your bike. In fact, if you are racing a time trial without tri-bars you are at a great disadvantage.

However, for a standard road bike it's best just to buy a normal set of handlebars. You can waste a lot of money on sophisticated equipment, and aerodynamics really only come into effect at high speed. If you do progress to buying a set, the best purchase is a set of clip-on tri-bars (though it is illegal to use tri-bars in road races). You don't need to change the head stem for these — simply clip them on. Leading manufacturers here are Scott and Profile of the US and, again, Cinelli.

OPPOSITE: **Tour de France champion in 1989, Greg LeMond was one of the first stars to use triathlon handlebars. In 1990, he came back with these Scott bars; the extended drops facilitated aerodynamics on descents.**

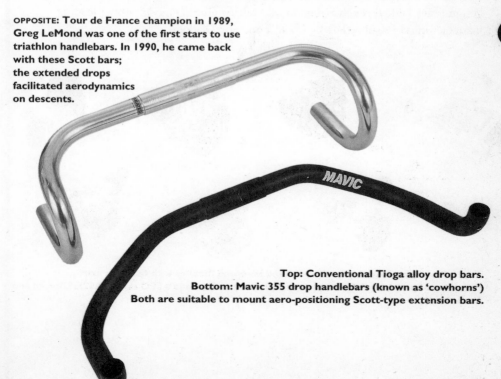

Top: **Conventional Tioga alloy drop bars.**
Bottom: **Mavic 355 drop handlebars (known as 'cowhorns')**
Both are suitable to mount aero-positioning Scott-type extension bars.

Pedals

As with many things in cycling, pedal choice is also a personal thing. The clipless pedal system comes in two versions: the Time model still allows for some movement of the foot when it is pushed into place, whereas the Look brand has cleats which are available with and without movement.

Riders usually prefer one or the other. Some people worry that at a crucial moment their foot will come out of a pedal which allows movement. And this can happen. But it has also been claimed that knee problems can result from using pedals with fixed cleats. Research by Time suggests that on the downward portion of a pedal stroke the foot has a natural tendency to move inwards and on the upward motion to move outwards. So in a clipless system, where there is no movement, ultimately the foot, leg, knee and tendons are all strained.

Shops do still sell the traditional toe-strap and cleat pedals, but they are generally regarded as obsolete nowadays. The only area where they are used is in track sprinting and by some purists in European six-day events and road-racing circuits.

Today most cyclists use a strapless click-in ski-binding system. Various materials are used, but cast aluminium is the most common. The benefit of this system is that you don't have the pressure of a strap around your foot which could cause irritation and cut off blood circulation. It also provides you with a more efficient foot position, enhancing pedal power because more of the foot is in contact with the pedal. (This type of pedal can also be used on mountain bikes, although the design is slightly smaller.) This design is available through Shimano who release an SPD model. Other leading manufacturers of road pedals are Look, Time and Diadora.

Top, left to right: Time Equipe Magnesium; Sampson Stratics with titanium axle; Primax road pedal; Look PP56; bottom, left to right: Shimano's SPD range: A525, Ultegra and Dura-Ace.

■ Cranks

Cranks are an important element to gearing. Young riders, juniors or newcomers to the sport should use shorter (170-millimetre) cranks. The purpose of having a longer crank is to ride a bigger gear. That means the revolutions will be less and more power is being used. Many professionals use 172.5 or 175-millimetre cranks, although some, like Miguel Induraín, use 180-millimetre. But not all riders have the ability to ride big cranks. There are very few Induraíns around!

Racing

How and Where to Start

So you want to race? Well, the most important first step is to join a cycling club. By doing this, not only will you get to race but you'll also find yourself amongst people who can advise you and expand your knowledge of almost every aspect of cycling.

To find out how to join a club, you could look in the telephone book for the nearest club or state or national cycling association number (*see Important Contacts on page 203*) or ask at your local bike shop. (In some cases the proprietor may also be a club sponsor and offer special discounts to all club members.) Another way of finding out this information is to ask cyclists you see on the road.

To join a club you will have to pay a membership fee and register with the local state or regional cycling association. Once you have signed up, there is an abundance of varying competition open to you — time trials, criteriums and short -circuit races, one-day road races and even stage races. Even if you don't want to compete, it's enjoyable belonging to a club because there are daily and weekend club runs to participate in as well as racing events.

When you begin racing you will start at a level of competition which matches your ability. As your results improve, you'll be scoring enough points to go up a grade and race against a higher level of competition. If you have the talent, rest assured the system will act fairly. In Australia, standards are set from D to A grades, with A grade being the élite. Countries like the United States and Great Britain follow a similar system, although they call their levels categories 4 to 1.

The Disciplines

Stage Races

These are events which consist of several races, from which the results are added together, the winner being the rider with the best time overall.

Stage races are also known as 'tours' and are designed to find the best all-rounder in the field. The winner does not necessarily win any section of the stage, but they must have the tactical awareness to realise when and where to make their biggest efforts, or when to conserve their energy.

A stage race usually pits riders against a variety of disciplines and terrain — sprints, mountains, time trials and flat stages. Most stage races include categories for the rider who excels in each discipline as well. So within the blue riband overall classification, there can be categories for best sprinter, climber and team.

The most famous of all stage races is the three-week Tour de France which usually consists of 21 or 22 stages. However, a stage race can also have as few as two or three stages.

One-day Mass Starts

A one-day mass start is simply a road race held on one day alone where all the riders start together in one bunch. The winner is the rider first across the finish line after completing the set distance.

Distances vary, depending on the terrain, the status of the event and the standard of entries. The longest events are generally 290 kilometres (180 miles) long and reserved for only the world's top professionals.

In longer races where the field might have a tendency to slow down and save their energies for the crucial kilometres near the end, it is not uncommon for an organiser to include several incentives for a faster pace along the way. These can include intermediate sprints or climbs where points are awarded for placings at those obstacles. These categories create a race within a race. Prizes are also offered for the best performing rider in these sections alone.

One-day races can also go from one city or town to another, although usually one-day races start and finish in the same town, with the route encompassing surrounding regions.

Handicaps

Handicap races are also held on one day, but with the field starting off at intervals, or waves, according to their ability. The least experienced riders start off first and the best riders start last, with a time handicap against them. They are called the 'scratchmen'.

Theoretically, the calculated time differences should see the field unite near the end. However, the variables in road racing — weather, terrain and tactics — often result in this not being the case.

29

ROAD CYCLING

Officially, the winner is the first rider across the line. However, most handicap races also include a category for the 'fastest' rider as well — i.e. the person who has covered the distance in the shortest elapsed time.

It is possible for a scratch rider to win outright. But they need to be incredibly strong and hope the riders they catch agree to work together in bunch formation to lessen the gap between the riders ahead of them.

Handicap racing is common in Australia, less so in the United States and Great Britain. While some people dislike it because it doesn't always see the best rider win, it is a great training opportunity for élite racers preparing for upcoming mass starts and stage races. It is also a way of having riders of varying standards compete against each other in one race.

Time Trials

This form of cycle racing bears two apt monikers: the Race of Truth, or Race Against the Clock. Time-trialling can be an individual or a team event.

In an individual race riders start at set intervals apart, and their result is the time taken to complete a set distance and course.

Time-trialling is unique in cycle racing because the rider is totally alone. When passed by another rider — or upon catching one — a time-triallist is not permitted to draw on that opponent's assistance by cycling in their slipstream or vice versa. A set distance must remain behind and next to every rider.

The same rules apply to team time trials as well, although members of a competing team are allowed to ride in formation, with riders taking turns at the front before dropping back and into the assisting slipstream of their team-mates.

Most time-trial races permit a team car to follow behind a rider or team. This is in case they need a wheel change or suffer a mechanical breakdown. Riders are also allowed to receive intermediate information about times and places from their team support.

Individual and team time-trialling events are often part of stage races and form the decisive elements in those races. There are also many time-trial events which are prestigious in themselves. In Europe, for example, there are such time-trial classics as the Grand Prix des Nations and the Grand Prix of Eddy Merckx. And in 1994 for the first time the individual time trial was included in the world championships (previously only team time-trialling was admitted as a category).

In Great Britain there is even a time-trial association called the British Best All Rounder (BBAR) which has a popular nationwide series of events ranging from distances of between 16 and 160 kilometres (10 and 100 miles) and times of up to 24 hours. Time-trialling is, of course, the key cycling discipline in triathlons where bike leg distances range from 30 to 180 kilometres (18 to 112 miles).

Greg LeMond
time-trials his way
to a record
0:08-second win
over Laurent Fignon
of France in the 1989
Tour de France on
the last stage.

Tactics

Climbing and Descending

These are two of the most important disciplines of road racing. They are also feats which conjure up the most fear in riders, as well as causing exhaustion.

As a result, they are two of the most spectacular activities to watch in cycling events, especially in stage races like the Tour de France, where up to 250 000 fans will congregate on a mountain slope to see riders suffer.

Stage races don't offer categories for best descender. If they did, the risks and accidents would be numerous. However, the focus on climbing is so great that there is a category for best climber and it is one of the most prestigious to achieve in any race.

Most people are born with a certain amount of climbing ability. However, while some cyclists prove to be natural climbers, it is possible for a rider with less climbing prowess to improve on their climbing ability. Be warned, though — there aren't any short cuts: it takes a lot of hard work on both conditioning and cycling skills. It is also a technique heavily dependent on an intelligent use of gears.

Generally speaking, there are two efficient ways to climb. Some riders climb sitting towards the back of the saddle, their hands gripping the top of the handlebars and legs pushing a low gear. Others find it better to ride out of the saddle, utilising a rocking motion with their shoulders. This is often called 'dancing' on the pedals and means that you are pulling up on the same side of the handlebars on which you are pedalling down.

What the technique of descending lacks in power and strength it makes up for in the need for nerves of steel and competence in bike handling. While climbs are often the launch pad for attacks in a race, it is on the descents that a poor climber can make up the time they have lost on the ascent.

The best position for descending is to get as close to a skier's tuck position as possible, with your hands on the drops, shoulders down towards the handlebars and elbows and knees brought in towards the torso.

Cornering while descending often catches riders out, simply because many people brake too often, especially with the rear brake, which has a tendency to cause the back wheel to skid out on a turn when used too severely.

Cornering

It can look dangerous but, with the right technique, cornering can be mastered — and it can even make the difference between winning and losing.

The basic principle to cornering downhill or on flat circuits is to take the most direct and straight line possible around a corner. The difference between cornering on a

**Italian Claudio Chiappucci,
King of the Mountains
in the 1992 Tour de France,
shows the benefit of sitting
at the back
of the saddle.**

The 1994 Tour de France passes over the French Alps. Here, riders in the main group ride together in tempo, their hope simply to make the finish within the time limit. Meanwhile, the race leaders — possibly kilometres away in front and in the throes of a gripping offensive — carry on the fight for the yellow jersey.

ABOVE: **Dane Johnny Weltz and his ONCE team-mates (in yellow) set the tempo at the front of the bunch in the 1992 Milan–San Remo classic.**
BELOW: **Frenchman Francois Simon outsprints Italian Massino Ghirolhi (left), Australian Neil Stephens (centre) and Adriano Baffi (right) to win a stage in the 1992 Tour of Italy.**

36

flat road and on a descent is that on a level surface you'll be going more slowly and will therefore have more time for correcting error.

Contrary to what a beginner may think, cornering is not about turning the handlebars around to the contours of the turn. Most beginners — and even some more experienced riders — make the mistake of racing towards a turn, braking at the last minute and then slowly negotiating a turn. Do that, and it will require a great amount of energy to accelerate to your previous speed again. Furthermore, it will give the bicycle a tendency to wobble out into the road and eventually leave you with lengths to catch up.

When approaching a turn, especially in a time trial, always look approximately 40 to 50 metres (44 to 55 yards) ahead — not directly in front. This helps you to pick a straight line to follow. On a descent, if it's possible, try to keep an eye out for the next couple of turns as well. This gives you more time to survey the road ahead for potential hazards like holes, loose debris, roadwork barriers or oncoming traffic.

When negotiating a turn, be prepared to drift out towards the side of the road opposite to the direction of that turn. Then, as the turn comes, lean the bike slowly, rather than abruptly, into the corner. When the corner is passed, allow the bike to roll out naturally in a straight line to the opposite side of the road again, rather than forcing it. Also be aware of others if you're cycling in a group.

Ideally, it's best not to brake on a turn. But if you do need to — for obvious reasons — begin the procedure before the actual corner arrives. Remember, though, never to slam on the brakes hard, as this will throw you off your bike (and probably bring down those following as well!). If you have to brake on the corner itself, try to use just the front brake — only squeezing it, so the deceleration is subtle, slow and under control.

In cycling generally, the less braking you do, the better. On a turn the greater the controlled speed, the greater the speed will be when you come out of it.

For uphill cornering, the shortest line theory is not always the best. Usually, on roads with a lot of hairpin bends and corners, the best place to ride is in the middle of the road. On the outside of an uphill hairpin, the gradient is always more gentle than on the inside. So you won't need to constantly get out of the saddle (which breaks up the rhythm); this technique can help a rider get to the top of the climb faster than any steeper 'short cuts' would.

Of course, if you're attacking on an uphill bend and you want to make a jump, you would want to take the inside of the turn, because that's the shortest way around it. Once you've got into the lead and settled into an even, attacking tempo, you would go back to the centre-road position.

Riding with experienced cyclists is a great way of learning the art of cornering. In time your 'feel' for cornering will develop, as too will a greater confidence in what can at first be a frightening and frustrating element of the sport.

38

■ Sprinting

This is also a spectacular part of racing. It involves explosive power, speed, tactical cunning and nerves of raw steel.

As with climbers, there are also born sprinters. But while climbers generally win in their domain by relying on their talents alone, a sprinter is heavily reliant on the cohesiveness of team-mates.

It is up to a sprinter's team-mates to muscle their way to the front of a speeding bunch, try to monopolise all the front positions and make sure he or she is tucked safely into their slipstream. Then, when the tempo speeds up under their acceleration, a sprinter will ride behind the front runners as they expend their energies for the finale. Finally, the sprinter goes all out for the finishing burst with 100 to 150 metres (109 to 164 yards) to go, in the hope that he or she will be the winner.

Belgian Eric Vanderaerden (middle) in a nail-biting sprint finish against Marcel Arntz (left) and Sean Kelly (right) in the 1989 Nissan Tour of Ireland.

Because every team normally has a sprinter, the congestion of riders at the front of a pack in the last kilometres can be frightening. At speeds of up to 60 kilometres per hour (kph) (37 miles per hour (mph)), and with only a centimetre or two between wheels, it takes only the slightest miscalculation or hesitation for cyclists to touch each other's wheels and fall down like dominoes.

As can be imagined, the build-up to a sprint finale and its explosive outcome is a major crowd-pulling aspect to any race.

Safety

Despite its pleasures and the physical well-being caused by cycling, the need for attentive safety measures when riding should never be ignored. As confidence on a bicycle grows — and inevitably speeds, difficulty of terrain and the standard of cycling company as well — so too do the risk factors. Do not become complacent.

The best professionals in the world can provide a frightening reminder of the hazards. To the most adoring cycling aficionados they may appear to be immortal in their feats, but they crash too!

Bike handling is a vital key to safe riding. And the best source of education here is to ride with experienced riders. Don't be afraid to ask for advice. Most people will freely give it. The best place for novice riders to learn is on bitumen roadways in closed park areas. In some cities and towns, bike lanes are commonplace, and they're a safer place to ride than the road.

Another factor is to learn the local road traffic rules wherever you are. Not only must cyclists abide by traffic legislation, but a basic knowledge of who has the right of way, for example, could help you to avoid a nasty collision. Also keep an eye open for the unpredictable behaviour of other cyclists or cars.

Wearing a helmet and brightly coloured clothing will improve your safety (see chapter 10 for advice on your cycling wardrobe).

Last, but not least, every cyclist should be prepared for the worst! Learning to anticipate a crash and how to fall are two elements which can minimise injury.

Dean Woods (right)
gives his German
team-mate Carsten
Wolf (left) a hand-sling
in a madison race
during the Bremen
Six-day event in 1992.

2 Track Cycling

Track cycling may not reap as much public attention in Europe as road racing, but to any converted cycling fan it is a fascinating element of the sport. It's not only thrilling to participate in but also gives you a superb education in bike handling and tactics. All cyclists will benefit from some form of track cycling, whether they focus on track racing or not.

Track cycling can take place on indoor and outdoor tracks, or velodromes. Velodromes differ in size and dimension and are made of varying materials, ranging from wood and cement to a combination of woods and synthetics.

Tactical instinct will need to be sharper because of the velocity of race patterns on the track. Leg speed will be much higher, yet at no cost — rather, benefit — to endurance. This will improve your road skills too, and the sport is full of many great track cyclists who have proved themselves as road stars as well.

Patrick Sercu of Belgium was one example. He was Amateur World Sprint Champion, an Olympic 'kilometre' gold medallist and then the greatest professional six-day rider ever. Yet he also won eight stages of the Tour de France, and the Tour's green points jersey.

On a more general front, track cycling is also a great spectator sport.

While road events like the Tour can cover up to 4000 kilometres (2485 miles), making it quite a logistical feat to witness, track competition is fought out in front of your eyes just as tennis is. This also makes it easier to cover on television, an important element in promoting the sport.

The flipside to the coin, though, is threefold: firstly, track cycling can at first appear to be a complicated thing to understand; secondly, it is a discipline which demands specific skills and steel nerves, and it can be more difficult to get into; and thirdly, construction of a velodrome is a costly affair which can limit the availability of facilities.

Nevertheless, any cyclist should not miss their first chance to either ride, race or watch a night of track racing. We can guarantee it won't be the last time you'll go!

Choosing
the **Right Bike**

To find the best track bike is an undertaking similar to choosing a road bike. However, you'll have fewer headaches as far as equipment is concerned, because there aren't so many components to a track bike — making them lighter and cheaper. And not only are there no brakes on a track bicycle, they also come equipped with only a fixed gear.

Positioning

To position yourself on a track bicycle, use the same procedure as for a road bicycle. If you already have a road bike, your position should be the same, even though a track bike's geometric design is different.

In some disciplines like pursuiting there may be cause for alterations, especially if you are using a revolutionary design. And when a novice becomes more experienced, he/she will notice slight positional variations (above the difference in frame designs) depending on the type of track event, and from this can make a more informed choice. However, beginners are best advised to stick to the basics and start with a traditional track bicycle.

single fixed gear

Anatomy

Frame angles in a track cycle are different. The fork rake — the bend in the lower part of the fork — is straighter (in road bikes it is angled to absorb the shock from bumps and holes). And the head column — the section of frame joining the head fittings with the forks — is normally much steeper on track bikes. This enhances the bike's responsiveness, a vital factor on tracks where lightning speeds and a tight circuit call for greater manoeuvrability.

The pursuit of aerodynamism has seen frame and wheel design and material undergo frequent and radical changes. So rapid have they been that the cycling world's governing body, the Union Cycliste Internationale (UCI), has been forced to

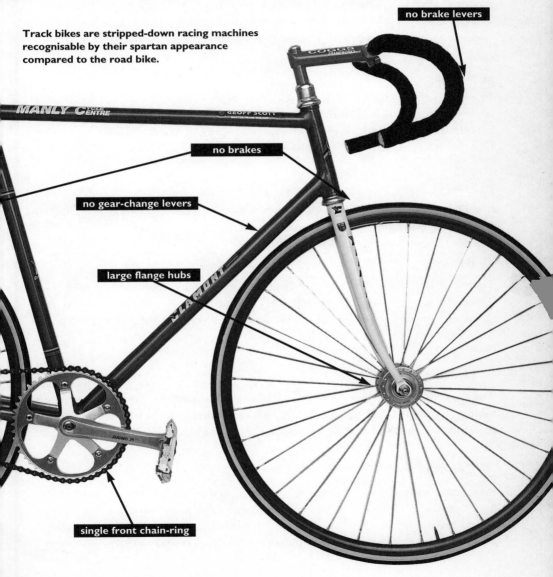

Track bikes are stripped-down racing machines recognisable by their spartan appearance compared to the road bike.

no brake levers

no brakes

no gear-change levers

large flange hubs

single front chain-ring

implement strict regulations. These have kept bicycle manufacturing and retailing costs within acceptable limits as well as establishing a more equitable level of competition where emphasis is on the person rather than the machine.

Wheels

Another difference between road and track machines is that track wheels have no quick-release system. And the spokes are often tied with fine grey fuse wire and soldered to give more strength. The use of disc wheels is also more popular nowadays.

Tyres

Track tyres are lighter too. A good track tyre is made of silk and cotton. (While good road tyres can be made of cotton, they have a heavier and thicker tread for the rougher conditions.) A recommended brand for singles is Continental from Germany and, for high-pressures, Michelin, Continental and Specialised.

Gears

Fixed gears are used in track racing because with a fixed gear you can pedal at higher revolutions for longer periods.

Brakes

There's no need for brakes in track bikes because on a velodrome, unlike a road, there are no obstacles to negotiate. To stop, track riders either roll to a halt during two or three warm-down laps, or a handler can take hold of a slowing rider's hand and pull him or her to a halt.

Handlebars

Track sprinters generally use rounded, chrome-steel handlebars. They are stronger and more comfortable to use than the traditional square design of the road bike, because track riders spend most of their time riding on the drops.

Cranks

Another difference between road and track bikes is that the latter has shorter cranks. Track cranks vary between 165 and 170 millimetres, whereas road cranks vary from 170 to 180 millimetres. And the chain width is 3 millimetres ($\frac{1}{8}$th inch) on a track bike compared to a slimmer 2.25 millimetres ($\frac{3}{32}$nd inch) on a road bike.

Racing

How and Where to Start

If the cycling club you have joined is a good one, then you should have access to a velodrome. Track cycling is, after all, a vital skill any rider should aim to learn whether they want to concentrate on track or road cycling.

If your club does not have access to track facilities, then — as with road cycling — ask your nearest cycling shop or contact any cycling magazine. Or you could ask a regional, state or national cycling federation to direct you to the most appropriate facility.

If you haven't cycled on a track before, remember to respect what more experienced people have to say or do.

The Disciplines

▮ Kilometre

The Kilometre is a demanding discipline where the rider is timed over a 1000-metre (1094-yard) track distance after a held start. The rider is forced to expend maximum energy from the gun. It's the ideal sprinters' time trial, requiring an extremely high anaerobic threshold and mental determination. Mechanical glitches or other misfortunes can cost a rider vital time at the beginning, but if all goes well many 'kilo' riders can achieve a good speed over the first 500 metres (547 yards). The top placings, however, are usually decided on who is strongest over the last half.

▮ Match Sprint

The Sprint is one of track cycling's most exciting events. A sprinter not only needs to be able to put on a burst of explosive speed, but he/she must also be cunning and opportunistic in what is as much a psychological as a physical battle.

Match Sprints pit two riders against each other. A rider's starting position is either close to the centre of the track or up on the bank. It is determined by drawing a ticket from a hat. What is considered the best position is a personal thing: some riders prefer the inside lane, starting from the front position; others like to begin from the

Englishman Chris Boardman winning the 1992 Olympic Games Pursuit title at Barcelona, Spain.

46

Scotland's Graeme Obree,
a long-time rival of Boardman's,
winning the 1993 World Open
Pursuit crown at Hamar, Norway,
on his notorious 'funny bike'.

outside and follow on. Once they have started, riders can change positions as often as they like.

The Match usually becomes a psychological game of 'cat and mouse'. In the preliminary laps accelerations and tactical moves up and down the bank are made by both riders to provoke the other into making a mistake. Another tactic is the 'stand-up', or track stand, where the rider will roll to a halt, balance and wait until either they or their rival takes off again. Physically, a stand-up can be painful after a period of time and can sap vital fast-twitch sprinting energy for the eventual sprint to come.

A crescendo of tension is created until one or the other finally launches the all-committed sprint to the line with about 200 metres (219 yards) to go. This final and decisive burst of speed can see riders edge frighteningly close to colliding, and sometimes they do. (Hence the need for steel nerves!)

Sprinters are often large and robust as a result of the weight work they do to increase muscle power. Not only are their legs huge, but so also are their shoulder and arm muscles, which are used a lot in accelerating.

▇ Tandem

The Tandem is like the individual Sprint, only much faster and more dangerous. Because there are two people on the bike, tactics like stand-ups are more difficult. Also, as there is a greater weight to wind up to the maximum speed, the finishing sprint often begins further from the finish than in the individual Sprint.

48

LEFT: **Italians Capitano and Paris make their jump on the Czechoslovak duo to clinch the 1992 World Tandem title at Valencia, Spain.** OPPOSITE: **Australia's 1992 Olympic Games silver-medal-winning team pursuit.**

Individual Pursuit

The Individual Pursuit is a race where two riders start off at either ends of the track —
one on the back straight and the other on the home straight. The aim of the race is for
one rider to try to catch the other.

If a rider is caught, they lose. If neither competitor is caught, the winner is the
rider with the fastest time for the 4000-metre (4374-yard) distance.

An Individual Pursuit series is normally made up of qualifying rides where a
cyclist completes the distance against another competitor. This is done to establish the
fastest and slowest riders and to work out match-ups for the first round. From there on
until the final, the series sees riders eliminated as they are beaten.

A pursuiter needs to have both speed and endurance. Such qualities also overlap
with other cycling disciplines like road time-trialling. It is not uncommon for pursuiters
to become excellent road racers as well.

A pursuiter should race with the
strategic cunning of a road cyclist too. They
can pinpoint the time they should need to
win and race to a schedule. Or, if their
opponent is an unknown quantity, they
could take a more confrontational approach
and try to scare him or her by blasting from
the starting line with added vigour in the
hope of unnerving their rival.

In the 1980s the former Soviet
Union and East Germany reigned supreme
as the world's best pursuiters, although the
early 1990s saw Great Britain and
Australia produce some excellent 'heirs'
to the former eastern bloc's throne.

Team Pursuit

The Team Pursuit is akin to individual
pursuiting, although it is a far more
visual spectacle.

Each race has two teams of four
riders. And, like the Individual Pursuit,
both teams start at opposite sides of
the track, with each aiming to catch
the other.

49

50

Points racing calls on many of the skills of road racing, with constant barrage attacks and chases, like those shown here in the 1992 World Professional Points Race title at Valencia, Spain.

If the teams don't catch each other, the result is decided on time which is measured when the third rider of each team finishes. This requires that all four riders try as much as possible to stay together and ride at an even tempo, rather than split up. It is usually with a couple of laps to go that a rider falls adrift after putting on a final extra turn of speed at the front.

Most 'turns' last half a lap, with the rider ending their spell at the front by sweeping up one of the two bankings and dropping down and behind the last rider in their team. While it was once regarded as impressive for strong riders to do one-lap turns, teams like the 1993 world champions — Australia — have riders who can produce two-lap turns!

Points Racing

The Points Race is an event in which points are awarded to the top five riders in sprints at allocated laps.

Of all the track events, it is this discipline which most requires the skill of road racing. The race is full of attacks, chases and official and secret alliances between riders.

Endurance, speed and pursuiting skills are major physical assets. Yet a points racer must also be able to 'read' a race well too. It is definitely an event where psychology, as well as strength, is a major factor.

In world championship competition women compete over 30 kilometres (18 miles). Up until the 1993 amalgamation of professional and amateur men's racing organisations there were 50-kilometre (31-mile) events for professionals and amateurs. Now, the new Open men's race is 40 kilometres (25 miles).

Teams for world-title and Commonwealth Games events can number two riders, whereas Olympic and Commonwealth Games competitions only allow for one rider per country.

Six-day Racing

Six-day racing originated in the United States, but has long found its base in Europe — especially in Germany.

Six-day Races used to last for the entire duration of six 24-hour days. Nowadays, however, this competition involves six nights of indoor racing between 8 p.m. and 3 a.m.

Unsurprisingly, the 'Sixes' are also major social events. While racing continues, paying visitors are provided with live music, restaurant and bar service and even access to on-site discos.

A Six-day meeting is a combination of numerous events contested by two-person teams. The overall winner is the team with the most laps or, if there are two or more teams with the same lap count, the winner is the one with the most points derived from intermediate sprints and bonuses.

The crucial event in a Six-day Race is the chase, or 'madison', where riders ignite attack after attack in bids to lap the field. (The name comes from its origins in Madison Square Gardens in New York.)

A madison requires both riders of a team to race, but they take it in turns and alternate every two or three laps by hand-slinging each other back into the thick of the action. The rider not racing rolls slowly around the top of the track, banking, until it is his or her turn to rejoin the race.

Distances vary, but can reach 75 kilometres (46 miles). Two races are usually held per night. Other components to a Six-day Race programme include motor-paced, intermediate sprint and elimination races. But they rarely carry the prestige of a madison, which will also appear in the World Championship programme in 1995.

Japanese Keirin

The Keirin is a special sprint event originating in Japan which has also been contested around the world under slightly different regulations.

In a Keirin race a field of about eight riders lines up and cycles the first laps behind a pacer. The aim of the pacer, who drops off with one lap to go before the finishing sprint, is to boost the pace of the race up to frighteningly fast levels. In a world-title programme, the pacer drives a motorbike. In Japan, where this type of cycling originated, the pacer rides a bicycle.

After trying to push and shove into the best positions, it is in this last lap that Keirin racers hit their peak as the full-out sprint to the line begins. Crashes are a common result.

In Japan, the Keirin is a lucrative, mass-marketed sporting institution which is open to legal betting, as horse and greyhound betting is in Australia, Great Britain and the United States.

There are official Keirin stadiums all over Japan and millions of dollars — or yen — pass hands between punters and bookmakers.

For those on the circuit, doors are only opened by invitation. Japanese riders must graduate to a competitor's class via strict and rigorous schooling.

Foreigners are also invited, but can only compete in an international round of races lasting three months from June. They, too, must go to 'Keirin school', but they're only required to attend a three-week crash course.

Motor-paced Racing

Motor-paced racing is also one of track cycling's more dangerous outlets. And it's one of the most demanding in terms of endurance.

Events usually last for about one hour. Each rider races behind a motorbike at speeds which can reach 80 kph (50 mph). Starting positions hinge on a pre-race draw and certainly affect one's chance of winning.

Tasmania's Danny Clark winning his second
World Professional Motor-paced title at
Stuttgart, Germany, in 1991.

Precise cohesion between the driver and
rider is vital, for a rider's intention of attacking or
passing an opponent depends on the driver being
able to accelerate and provide the extra slipstream
when the rider needs it.

Like the Tandem , motor-paced racing was
a world-title event for professionals and amateurs
until 1993. Sadly, despite the athletic prowess
needed to win a Motor-paced Race, such racing
has become something of a black sheep in the
flock of track cycling.

The deafening noise of accelerating
motorbikes is a contributing factor to its decline in
favour. A separate winter circuit in Europe helps to
further marginalise the event's identity. And being
allied to other events — such as the world titles —
only once a year doesn't help its popularity.

Safety

There are dangers associated
with track racing which you
should be aware of if you're not
properly acquainted with riding
on a velodrome. Your coach
should educate you on the
decorum of track rules, as well
as teaching you track-riding skills.
The most basic of all rules is to
remember that someone may be
riding right behind you. So
always keep an eye on what is
behind and around you. And
when you are in a bunch
situation and decide to drop off
the front and go to the rear,
always sweep up the bank and to
the right, rather than down and
towards the centre pit area.
As with road cycling, it is
essential to make sure that your
equipment is in good condition
before riding. Not only are you
taking measures for your own
safety, but also that of others
riding with you.

TRACK CYCLING

3 Cycling Alternatives

There's much more to cycling than road and track racing. Although they are the traditional competitive outlets to the sport, there's still a variety of cycling alternatives.

Mountain biking is the foremost amongst these choices today. Cycle touring has long been a favourite of passionate cycling enthusiasts. And there are even more adventurous forms of cycling such as cyclo-cross and triathlon, not to mention cyclo-ball and artistic cycling!

Mountain Biking

Of all the cycling possibilities, mountain biking is growing fastest in popularity, participation and on the commercial front.

Mountain biking originated in the United States in the 1980s, and mountain bikes are now seen and ridden throughout the world, both recreationally and competitively. This wave of interest has seen the sport become a manufacturer's and advertiser's paradise.

Competitively, it's a taxing sport, needing strong endurance and a high anaerobic threshold. Mountain biking is also a popular form of off-season or alternative training for athletes in other fields.

Recreationally, mountain biking is popular because of the simple fact that the bicycle itself is easier to balance and has a wider range of facilitating gears. As a result, for the beginner, mountain biking is a safer and more accessible form of cycle sport for a wider cross-section of ages.

Mountain bikes are practical bicycles for the inner-city as well, as they can not only weave through traffic jams, but also alleviate the need for the parking space which cars need. Commuters who live on the outskirts of major cities or congested business districts often find them an ideal form of transport to and from work. And even within the city, mountain-bike courier services are becoming increasingly more popular as — unlike cars or vans — they can negotiate city traffic much more quickly and more directly. And there's the attraction of mountain biking's adventuristic off-road nature. No longer do people have to equate cycling with dangerous traffic hazards and bitumen roads. With a mountain bike, one can ride on dirt trails, across grass and almost anywhere.

When mountain bikes first hit the market, they appeared cumbersome objects. Many purists laughed at them until bicycle manufacturers refined design, weight and the attached components. Today a mountain bike is a relatively slick racing machine and a product of as much technological development as are road or track bicycles.

However, there are still enough differences to make the mountain bike unique.

Anatomy

Frames

Mountain-bike frames are generally oversized, or fatter, than road and track frames. And they come in all types of material — carbon-fibre, kevlar, titanium, aluminium and steel. Because of the sport's nature, a mountain-bike frame needs to be strong and durable.

Top professionals can afford to sacrifice durability for added lightness but, as a first-time buyer, it's advisable to attend to durability first — you'll get better value for your money.

Wheels

Mountain-bike wheels are also different. You can buy lightweight rims and tyres which are not much heavier than those used on the road and track, with the added advantage that they are wider and sturdier. And the tyres will have a raised design on them to grip the often rocky terrain a mountain bike is ridden over.

Lightweight wheels are expensive. So if you're starting out mountain biking, it's best to save your money by avoiding high-tech material for now, and concentrate on buying less expensive wheels which are still good-quality; some examples of these are Araya, Ritchey and Mavic.

▇ Forks and Suspension

Most forks are made of aluminium, though many mountain bikes come equipped (or can be supplied) with a front suspension system which absorbs the shock from riding over rough terrain. Recently, read-end suspension systems have also been developed. One of the most popular brands — and the first to appear — is Rock Shox, from the US.

flat handlebars

handlebar-mounted gear shifters

cantilever brakes

rear suspension

front suspension

knobby tyres

triple front chain-rings

26" rims

■ Gears

An obvious difference in a mountain bike is that there are more gears. Mountain bikes generally come equipped with 21 gears, with three front chain-rings of 26, 36 and 48 teeth, or sprockets, and a rear 'block', or cluster, with a gear ratio of 12 to 30 sprockets.

■ Brakes

Brake systems are cantilever-designed — that is, the brake blocks are pulled by a cable attached to the brake lever. The greater clearance between wheel and brake helps to prevent the brakes becoming blocked up with mud and dirt as might be the case with more modern dual side-pull brake systems which are now common with road bikes.

■ Handlebars

One of the most obvious differences between mountain bikes and road or track bikes is the handlebars. These are T-shaped and wider than those on a road bike in order to absorb the shock from uneven surfaces and to provide the rider with greater control and more effective leverage for uphill sections. An average width is 52 centimetres (20½ inches) with the stem being a touch longer too. An assortment of handlebar extensions are available which facilitate climbing.

■ Pedals and Cranks

58

The pedal and crank system of a mountain bike seems at first glance to be the same as a road bicycle. However, there are subtle differences. Cranks are longer to provide more leverage on steep hills. An average mountain-bike crank is about 175 millimetres (6⅞ inches) long.

And while they can come equipped with standard pedals, a special clipless design has been created just for mountain bikes. Clipless pedals are used on road bikes too, but the mountain-bike version is designed to fit a special mountain shoe. Like a road-cycling shoe, it has a stiff inner sole to enhance pedalling efficiency. It also has a relatively thick rubber outer sole to help the rider to walk or run with the bike.

Racing

Competitively, mountain biking has rocketed in stature since its origins. In 1996 it will even be an official sport in the Olympic Games at Atlanta! Now affiliated with the Union Cycliste Internationale, mountain biking has a full international racing calendar leading up to that Olympic target.

Nearly every UCI-registered country has mountain-bike racing. On a global front, the key circuits are the Grundig World Cup and annual World Championships. In Europe there are also annual European titles. And there are many domestic national series like those which exist in Australia, the United States and Great Britain.

There are two main types of mountain-bike-racing — the individual cross-country event, which usually lasts about two hours and is held on a circuit (it is this event which has been included in the Olympic Games programme), and the downhill time trial, where riders are timed over the distance, the winner being the rider with the fastest time.

As with road and track racing, mountain-bike competition is open to a variety of categories from beginners to élite professionals who can earn up to A$500 000 a year!

Tactics

Because mountain biking takes place off the road, both cross-country and downhill racing can be dangerous — unlike recreational mountain biking. It is a discipline which requires incredible bike-handling skills. If you don't have them, don't worry — you'll develop them after several races.

In mountain biking, sprinting is not a vital element. So much relies on climbing and descending that a mountain-bike race very rarely climaxes with the sprint finishes you see in road racing. If ever there is a sprint, it is usually between two or three riders at the most. And while there is a sprinting acceleration, it is more a surge of pure power than the tactical cunning and bike-handling skill you find in road racing.

60

Climbing and Descending

These are the two main skills behind mountain biking.

When climbing you generally spend more time in the saddle than you would on a standard road bike, although this can vary depending on your own preferences and ability.

You might find yourself standing up on the pedals in steeper sections. But remember that by staying seated and pedalling with a low gear on longer climbs (and thus saving energy), you stand more chance of making it to the top.

If you feel you are not going to make the climb without stopping, it's best to dismount earlier rather than later. If you wait until you can't pedal any more and you are on a steep section, there is the chance you will topple over. By halting earlier, on a flatter section, you may be able to dismount and continue running with the bike until you find an easier gradient.

If ascending is a question of endurance and basic skill, descending requires raw courage and an ice-cool attitude to the task ahead.

The speed factor and unpredictable ground ahead of you require quick thinking.

Although beginners should take any descent cautiously, experienced racers learn to rely on instinct.

For both beginners and more experienced racers, there are several key skills to descending.

Firstly, one should remain relaxed, even though this may seem a tough task to begin with! A tense position and grip on the handlebars not only creates added fatigue and minimises your recovery from a climb, it can also limit your agility and potential to adapt to the varying terrain ahead of you.

The best thing to do on any descent is to keep your body weight as far back as possible, yet without hanging over the back wheel. Sit at the back of the saddle or out of it, standing on the pedals only. This helps to spread the vibration from your legs, lower back and hips to your arms, hands and upper torso. Your entire body becomes a veritable shock absorber!

Always keep a finger on the brake lever. But never brake too suddenly or too hard. Try to be subtle with the brakes and squeeze them, rather than pull on them. And try not to use the front brake too much because this will hinder manoeuvrability, and will very likely increase the odds of you projecting yourself from the bike like a rocket missile!

Cyclo-cross

Cyclo-cross is another off-road alternative, though it has a longer heritage than mountain biking.

Its origin was in Belgium as a form of off-season training for road racers. As training spins became harder and harder, they turned into races. In 1910 Belgium staged its first national cyclo-cross championship which was won by Philippe Thijs, the Tour de France champion in 1913, 1914 and 1920.

It took 40 years for cyclo-cross to become a world-championship event. When it did, in 1950, the first title-holder was 1947 Tour champion, Frenchman Jean Robic. Cyclo-cross was still very much dominated by the road racers.

Today, however, cyclo-cross is more specialised. It is no longer a source of off-season training, but a form of cycle-sport in itself which requires a composite make-up of road racing and running endurance skills.

Not only are there world championships, but now there are also two international series in the European Super Prestige and World Cup circuits and an official world-ranking system. What's more, there are national championship and domestic circuits in Belgium, France, Holland, Italy, Spain, Luxemburg, Great Britain and the United States. Sadly, in Australia the sport does not exist. Up until 1966 the World Championship was 'open' for amateurs and professionals. From 1967 to 1993 there were separate championship races for both categories. In 1994 the championship was once more contested as an open race.

Cyclo-cross races last about an hour and cover specially selected circuits which vary in terrain and challenge. Racing involves a mix of both cycling and running. Like mountain biking, the variety of obstacles means you need good bike-handling skills and a daring opportunistic streak to take advantage of attacks.

Some courses are slow and either extremely wet, muddy or sandy. Here cyclo-cross racers can often find themselves running with the bike on their shoulder. Other circuits can be dry, hard and fast and require very little running. Yet almost all courses include deliberately placed rises and descents and a variety of obstacles ranging from wooden metre-high hurdles to a series of steps constructed from wooden logs.

Anatomy

Frames

At first glance the cyclo-cross bicycle looks similar to a road bicycle. There are distinct differences, though, the main one being that a cyclo-cross frame is longer and has greater clearance around the various joins. This stops mud from getting blocked in between wheel and frame.

Wheels

Cyclo-cross tyres have knobbled treads which help traction over mud or dirt. Hubs are generally small flange and rims come equipped with 36 spokes for greater strength.

Gears

Speed is necessarily much slower than in a road race so cyclo-cross bikes are equipped with lower gears. In cases where a section of the circuit includes bitumen, riders might add a 14-tooth gear to provide added acceleration and speed.

Gear levers are normally placed at the end of the handlebar drops — and not on the down tube, as on a road bike.

Brakes

As in mountain bikes, cyclo-cross bikes have centre-pull cantilever brake systems. These are light, strong and, most importantly — unlike the dual side-pull system — are unlikely to clog up with mud because of the larger spacing they have between the brake and wheel.

Former world cyclo-cross champion
Radomir Simunek on his way to second place
in the World Cup round at Eindhoven,
Holland, in October 1993.

CYCLING ALTERNATIVES

Daniele Pontoni, the 1994 Italian cyclo-cross champion, and one of the world's biggest cyclo-cross stars, typifies the method of carrying a bike during the running sections of a race.

■ Saddles and Handlebars

The only real difference in riding position from a road bike is that the cyclo-cross saddle may be slightly lower and the handlebars slightly raised.

■ Pedals

Most cyclo-cross riders use double-strapped systems. Single straps can break, whereas the now common clipless system in road and mountain bikes can easily see feet slip out if used in a cyclo-cross race. However, mountain bike shoes with rubber/plastic outer soles are popular as they are good for running.

Randonnées

Europe is the heartland of the randonnée. The aim of a randonnée is pleasure, and along a route you might see riders stopping off at roadside beer tents, wine-tastings or barbecues.

You can also ride competitively in a randonnée. In France, there is even an official circuit of randonnées, where regular participants are awarded points according to their performances.

Cyclists pay to ride a marked route, which can include sections of some of the most famous races in the world, giving the cycling aficionado a first-hand experience of the terrain their idols compete on.

Randonnées are often named after former champions or historic events. Examples include Le Bernard Hinault, after the five-times French Tour de France winner who retired in 1986; Le Louison Bobet, after a three-times Tour winner from France; Le Flechette, after the hilly Belgian one-day classic, the Flèche–Wallonne; and l'Etape du Tour, which covers a chosen stage of each year's Tour de France the day before the actual race tackles it.

Before starting a randonnée, each rider is given a card which must be stamped and signed at each checkpoint on the route. Entrants are allowed to start whenever they like, within a certain time block. Their starting time is written on the card and, as long as every checkpoint has been passed, a time for completing the distance is recorded.

Competitive riders normally start first and organisers present an official winner's trophy to the first finisher of the day. It is not uncommon for amateur clubs, or competitive triathletes and mountain bikers to use randonnées as a form of extra competitive training. It has even been known for some regular winners to become professional road racers.

Audax

The Audax is a world-wide cycling association whose members endeavour to ride certain distances which are officially recorded and timed.

An Audax ride is different from a randonnée or community fun ride in that it is made independently, although officially recorded. To register a distance attempt, the cyclist must have the route planned and a certain number of Audax-approved author-ities on hand to witness and register their passage through various checkpoints.

Touring

The 1987 Tour de France winner, Stephen Roche of Ireland, aptly summed up the role cyclo-tourism has to play in the sport when he said, 'You haven't experienced cycling until you have done cyclo-tourism.'

Such words were surprising, considering they came immediately after his victory in the world's toughest and most prestigious race. But in every way what he says is true. For cyclo-touring is a sport designed simply for pleasure and with no relationship to the world of recorded times and distances.

Cyclo-tourism is what it says it is — a way of discovering the surrounding country side by bicycle. Its origins come from a time in many people's childhood when they would meet up with friends, take a back-pack with food and pedal off for the day. It was this fond memory Roche was talking about when he spoke in 1987.

There are now many holidays designed especially for cyclo-tourists, with rides to vineyards and farms, for example.

Other trips, particularly in Europe, include bike tours to some of the great cycle races like the Tour de France. These

luggage rack

groups ride on or close to the route, see the event go past and cycle on to a pre-booked hotel or guest house for the night. They are usually followed by back-up cars and/or vans in case anyone feels they've had enough and would prefer a lift.

Anyone can organise their own cyclo-tour. It's a good idea to contact a local cycling association for advice, though, on how to be best prepared.

generous size seat

behind-seat carry bag

emergency hand pump

down-tube gear levers

heavily spoked wheels

triple front chain-wheel

cage pedals

Community
Fun Rides

The spirit of a community fun ride is similar to a randonnée, although far less competitive. It's similar to a fun run, although on wheels. In most cases all proceeds from the entries are given to charity.

The main difference between a community ride and a randonnée is that the community ride start is en masse and the number of participants can be greater than in a randonnée, with up to 80 000 entrants!

There are many great community rides around the world. In Australia there is the Great Victorian Bike Ride and in Great Britain the most famous is London–Brighton.

You don't need to be registered with a club to join these events, which are usually widely publicised in the local print and electronic media.

However, most events require that entrants wear helmets.

Other **Alternatives**

Triathlon

This competition — where a cycling leg is sandwiched between swimming and running — is a rapidly developing event in Europe, America and Australasia. Although it's not affiliated with the UCI, triathlon competitions have had an enormous impact on the growing interest in cycling

It is a form of competition which boasts a feast of international competition and there are national series in most countries. For the top professionals there are various international circuits like the International Triathlon Union's (ITU) World Cup and the World Ironman Circuit where races cover 3.8 kilometres (2.4 miles) of swimming, a 180-kilometre (112-mile) bike ride and 42.2 kilometres (26.2 miles) of running. The circuit climaxes in Hawaii every October with the Hawaii Ironman.

An international winter indoor circuit is also being planned. And in 1994 it was ratified as an official Olympic sport for the 2000 Games in Sydney after its exhibition staging at Atlanta in the United States in 1996.

Australian Greg Welch leads Brad Beven in the Geelong leg of the 1993 Tooheys' Blue Triathlon series. In October 1994, Welch, a former world triathlon and duathlon champion, made history when he became the first non-American to win the Hawaii Ironman Triathlon.

rear disc aero wheel

Duathlon

Called by some a triathlon for those who can't swim, the duathlon is a cycle time trial sandwiched between two running legs. Distances vary from the sprint course of 40 kilometres (made up of 5 kilometres' running, 30 kilometres' cycling, and 5 kilometres' running), to the 13, 150 and 30-kilometre course of the Zofingen Powerman Duathlon held in Switzerland. Popular amongst triathletes during the winter months, duathlon also has a professional International series under the control of the ITU, culminating in an annual World Championship event.

A second international circuit emerged in 1994 — the Powerman series — with events in 11 countries world wide acting as qualification races for the tough Zofingen Duathlon.

forward mounted gear-change levers

elbow support pads

adjustable head stem

cow-horn handelbars

AEROVantage

clip-on aero bars

carbon-fibre monocoque frame

deep-rimmed aero wheel

high-pressure tyres

clipless pedals

4 Body
Maintenance

It's a well worn-sporting adage that mind should prevail over body. In many ways it's true but, no matter how much a cyclist — or any athlete for that matter — wants to produce their best, they will not do so without a thorough, well-planned approach to body maintenance.

There are many facets to body maintenance. They include diet, massage and stretching, vitamin and mineral supplement intake and first aid.

This chapter explains the basic elements to body maintenance. It also outlines the most important theories behind the bodily demands for better performance.

Australian professional Scott Sunderland receives treatment for a crash wound during the 1993 Tour of Spain.

Diet

A cyclist needs a well-balanced diet to enhance physical development, create energy and boost recovery. Disregard for nutrition will only lead to a downfall in performance.

Yet at the same time the intake should not overtake the requirements. If it does, then body fat will build up.

There are six main nutrients to consider: protein, minerals, vitamins, carbohydrates, fats and water.

However, it is not that simple to find an adequate balance of them in today's foodstuffs. Many foods are processed and contain colouring, flavouring and preservatives.

Energy is derived from proteins, fats and carbohydrates — these are called energy nutrients.

Ideal sources for vitamins and minerals are fresh fruits and vegetables in either whole or juice form.

Protein is mainly derived from meat which also provides minerals and vitamins. However, red meat should be eaten in limited quantities. Other sources include dairy products, eggs, bread and cereals, soya beans, red and white beans, peas and nuts.

And when a cyclist is on a rigorous training programme glucose and fructose supplements are needed which help supply extra energy without overloading the digestive system with excessive food. An ideal substance is honey, which is full of fructose, water, vitamins, minerals and carbohydrates.

74

Norwegian pro Dag-Otto Lauritzen shows what he will eat during a typical day of the Tour de France.

Body fat can be an energy source, but it is not easy to draw on. Normally it is only accessed when glucose stores are drained. Not only are there various methods to measure body fat, but the levels also vary between males and females and between road and track cyclists.

In cycling, road riders generally have a lower level of body fat than track riders. And while the average body-fat percentage for a male would be 15% — as against a 23%-level for a female — an average body-fat percentage for a male rider would be between 5 to 8%, with female riders again having a proportionally greater level.

What the Nutrients Do

It's all very well to hear or read about what nutrients a cyclist needs and where they come from. But to help understand how the body works and reacts, it is also important to understand what they do.

▇ Carbohydrates

These give energy and heat to the body during exercise. They are a far better energy source of fuel than fat, as they require less oxygen to produce the same amount of energy.

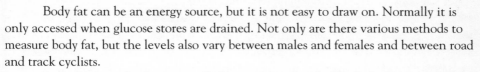

75

Carbohydrates come from plant foodstuffs like grains, vegetables and fruit. They come in simple and complex forms. Simple carbohydrates include the sugars glucose, fructose and galactose. They are absorbed by the system and can be used immediately for energy or stored for later use as glycogen. Complex carbohydrates are the 'double' sugars, or disaccharides, such as sucrose and maltose, and polysaccharides like starch and glycogen.

All carbohydrates need to be broken down to simple sugars by digestion before they can actually be absorbed by the system. Only a limited amount can be stored as glycogen in the liver and muscles.

Sugars

When digestion occurs, sugars go to the bloodstream and then to the organs and tissues needing them, like the brain, liver and nervous system. Stored as glycogen, they are used whenever muscle contraction occurs.

The liver stores glucose for energy production. So whenever the glucose level in the blood drops, it is rapidly replenished from those stores of glycogen in the liver. When sugar levels drop in the brain, mental efficiency is reduced. The risks of sugar levels dropping increase as a rider uses more energy. It is estimated that the average length of time that the body can endure strenuous exercise without sugar levels being reduced to this level is $1\frac{1}{2}$ hours, so cyclists must be prepared to replenish their levels accordingly.

Fats

76

Fats fulfill a similar task to sugars in releasing energy and they help the system to absorb fat-soluble vitamins.

However, they shouldn't be consumed just before a race because they are harder to digest. They also have 50% more calories per kilogram than carbohydrates and proteins. So if you consume too much fat and don't do enough exercise, your body weight will increase.

Fats exist in two forms: **unsaturated**, which are found in vegetable oils and **saturated**, which are found in all animal oils except fish and poultry. Natural sources of both forms of fats are milk, meat, egg-yolk, nuts, butter, cream and salad oil.

Water

Water makes up the main component in the body and comes from both the food and fluid we consume. Research shows that 50 to 70% of our body is water. Any significant reduction of water reduces the supply of blood to the muscles, which finally affects performance.

During a race, riders must re-fuel while they can.

It is essential that any cyclist maintains fluid intake while racing and training. In hot conditions, the body weight of an endurance cyclist can fall by 8% due to sweat loss alone. And it takes only a 3% weight loss for an increase in heart rate and body temperature to occur. The same loss can drastically reduce muscular exertion by up to 30%!

Proteins

These are important for boosting muscle-tissue strength and fluid levels after a hard training session or race. They can also be used to create antibodies against viruses and bacteria. They are not a major energy source, although they can be broken down into fuel after all carbohydrates are drained. They should make up between 12 to 17% of a cyclist's diet, according to an individual's growth and energy output.

Vitamins

Vitamins are essential for the chemical reactions which keep the body in working order. Vitamins can be either fat or water-soluble. Fat-soluble vitamins are stored by the body in large quantities, water-soluble vitamins in small quantities.

As already mentioned, processed foods may not provide the vitamin supply your body needs. Illness or rigorous training, too, may lead to a need for vitamin supplements. The main vitamins are vitamins A, B1 Thiamine, B2 Riboflavin, B3 Nicotinamide, C and D.

Vitamin A is found in milk, butter, egg-yolk, carrots, green vegetables, fish oils and liver. Its benefits include maintaining healthy skin and hair, good eyesight and a resistance to conjunctivitis and other infections. Hints of any deficiency include dry, rough skin, respiratory soreness and night blindness.

Vitamin B1 Thiamine comes from wholegrain cereals, wheatgerm, fish, pork, lean meat, milk and potatoes. It produces enzymes which release energy from blood glucose, thus maintaining the sound functioning of the heart and nervous system. Lack of energy, fatigue and loss of appetite are key signs of the inadequate supply of this vitamin.

Vitamin B2 Riboflavin exists in wheatgerm, bread, cereals, green vegetables, lean meat, liver, dried yeast, milk and eggs. It helps cells use oxygen, builds body tissue, keeps skin healthy and minimises the sensitivity of eyes. It is thought that this vitamin helps to combat disease, cracked lips and inflamed eyelids.

Vitamin B3 Nicotinamide is found in dried yeast, eggs, liver, fish, lean meat, bread and cereals. It helps riders to keep their appetite, converts food into energy, helps the nervous system and enhances the release of energy from food. Indigestion and fatigue are deficiency signs here.

Vitamin C is found in citrus fruits, tomatoes, green vegetables, strawberries, broccoli and potatoes. It is helpful in boosting resistance to infection, strengthening teeth, bones, gums, body tissues and blood vessels; it creates collagen (a protein substance which binds body cells) and promotes the healing of broken bones and wounds. Signs of vitamin C deficiency include increased vulnerability to infection, sensitive gums, mild anaemia and slow healing of wounds.

Vitamin D exists in cod-liver oil, salmon, tuna, egg-yolk, milk and butter. It is beneficial in aiding the transport of calcium and phosphorous into the bloodstream and from there into the marrow cells. Deficiency leads to reduced bone marrow growth.

Minerals

These come in various forms. Up to 20 minerals are needed by the body, the main ones being calcium, iron, sodium, potassium and phosphorous.

Calcium helps maintain strong bones and teeth, aids blood clotting after any injury and helps muscle recovery. Calcium sources include milk, cheese, peas, beans, yoghurt and wholegrain cereals.

Iron with protein creates haemoglobin to carry oxygen to the red blood cells, preventing anaemia. Women are more likely to suffer from a deficiency because of blood loss in their monthly period. Iron is found in liver, leafy vegetables, dried fruit, meat and eggs.

Sodium controls water levels in the body and helps muscle contraction. When deprived of sodium, a person can suffer from muscle cramps. It is found in most foods.

Potassium helps regulate the heartbeat and blood pressure during competition. It is also important for regulating acid base and water content in the cells and setting off muscle contraction in the transmission of nerve impulses. Food sources of potassium include milk, wheatgerm, bran and dried fruit.

Phosphorous metabolises vitamins and minerals. It is also an element in creating strong bones and tooth structure. It is present in meat, fish, poultry, eggs, cereals and nuts.

Losing Weight

To lose body fat, a diet is vital. However, just as important is a well-planned exercise programme.

To be effective, both steps must begin well before racing. This will give you time to invest in slow, long-distance work while the body simultaneously adapts to its new weight. Dramatic short-term weight losses will not only be temporary, but can also damage health.

A Recommended Procedure for Losing Weight

- Work out how many kilograms (or pounds) need to be lost.
- Divide this figure by 0.75 (for kilograms) or 1.6 (for pounds) to come up with the number of weeks that will be needed to lose the weight.
- Calculate the required kilojoule/calorie intake to maintain your current body weight.
- Cut that figure by 3140 kilojoules (for kilograms) or 750 calories (for pounds) per day and eat accordingly.
- Follow progress.

Eating: Before, During and After Competition

Before

Carbohydrate loading is the technique used by cyclists before an event to stock up on fuel. This fuel comes from carbohydrates and fats. Carbohydrates are stored as glycogen in muscle cells and the liver; fats exist as triglycerides in tissue and muscle.

In endurance events, fuel is burnt up by oxygen. Long-distance racers require an average store of 5000 to 8000 calories. The need for replenishment is important here as the body can only ordinarily store 2000 to 4000 calories as glycogen.

Carbohydrate loading can start a week before the event. Begin the process by going for a long ride. This will reduce your body's glycogen stores. To keep them depleted, follow a low-carbohydrate diet for three to four days and continue training. Then switch to a high carbohydrate diet for the three to four days before the event. The body will respond by overloading the system after earlier being deprived of an adequate supply of carbohydrates.

However, caution is called for when using this procedure. Muscle heaviness can occur. And some riders experience negative side effects.

When race day arrives, nutrition should be considered carefully. Nerves can affect your digestive system, and foods which are hard to process will stay in the stomach longer. To help digestion, remember that small pieces of food will help the process, and avoid spicy food.

Timing a pre-race meal is vital too. It's best to eat more food for longer, endurance events, while short races require less food. Whatever the distance you are racing, eating slowly helps digestion. The longer you set aside for eating, the more you can eat. It's best to eat a moderate-sized meal two and a half to three hours before racing.

Below are some examples of pre-race meals and when to eat them:

4–5 hours before: moderate portions of lean meat, potato, corn, peas and rice
3 hours before: small serving of fish, boiled potato, rice, fruit, bread and cake
2 hours before: fruit or vegetable juices, rice with glucose, bread and cake
1 hour before: fruit or vegetable juices, glucose in fluid, chocolate

During

The body will not only lose carbohydrates during a race, but also minerals, water and vitamins. So it is necessary to keep their respective levels up during any competition.

Sports drinks are a must
for any cyclist — pro or not.

When you lose water, the blood supply loses it as well, with the result that the heart is called on to work harder to transport oxygen and nutrients through the body.

To avoid this process, drink regular small quantities of water throughout an event. This will top up the already hydrated system immediately. Once the process of dehydration starts, it's an almost unwinnable fight to beat it.

The loss of carbohydrates is generally known as 'hunger flat', or 'the bonk' in the United States.

To keep glucose levels up during the race, many people use glucose 'sports drinks'. These drinks replenish lost vitamins, minerals and water. They can come in sugar-concentrated liquid, although this form of glucose isn't recommended because sugar can impede the flow of fluids into the system.

Some recommended brands of sports drinks include Gatorade, Isostar, Extran and Exceed.

The cyclist can choose either water or a sugar-concentrated drink — or go for both, with two 'bidon' cages for each type of drink. If you're sweating heavily, though, water should be the priority. If heavy sweating is not apparent, then a glucose fluid is ideal.

Whatever you do, the rate of fluid loss during competition is usually greater than you can compensate for. In one hour of competition, the stomach can only release about 800 millilitres (1¾ pints) of ingested fluids into the system; natural losses, on the other hand, are about two and a half times that level.

Beware, too, of the dangers of drinking *too much* fluid during competition — that is, more than 800 millilitres an hour. This will lead to stomach troubles and, obviously, impairs performance.

82

After

It's best to wait for at least an hour after competition before eating anything substantial. Your priority should be to replace lost nutrients with liquid-based substances, because these can be absorbed more quickly.

Certain foods should be avoided if competition is scheduled again for the next day. Foods which are easily digested are recommended. Suggested types include: cream and butter for fat needs; bread, puddings and rice for carbohydrates; fruit and juices for vitamin C and as a liquid nutrient replacement.

Massage
and **Stretch**ing

Massage and stretching are important elements in both the preparatory and recovery phases of a cyclist's training. They help the muscles to relax and warm up before an event and rejuvenate their strength and suppleness after a hard training session or race.

Massage

The regular use of massage by cyclists is one of the reasons that they shave their legs: smooth legs make massage easier for the masseur and less painful for the rider. (Another benefit of shaving is that cuts and grazes will heal more quickly and cleanly on shaven legs. If hairs become congealed in a wound, they can cause infection.)

If you do want to shave your legs, use a sharp razor — but carefully — and shaving cream. It's a good idea to wash your legs thoroughly with soap afterwards to avoid any nicks or cuts from the process becoming infected. Cyclists usually shave their legs once or twice a week because unless you do it regularly, hair grows back more quickly.

(There's also a supposed aerodynamic benefit to shaving legs. Cyclists have long done it and it is regarded as 'tradition'. But the time advantage it would bring, if any, would be more apparent on the track or in time-trial events, than in a road race.)

The cost factor of massage can be a problem for cyclists. If this is the case, you'll have to forego regular sessions and concentrate on pre and post-race massage. An important rule to follow is to make sure your masseur is qualified because by having a massage from an unqualified person, you will run the risk of incurring an injury. Qualified masseurs are trained in the art of giving massage and, importantly, in sensing which muscles, tendons and ligaments need it. (A masseur who is not properly trained could locate the wrong area of treatment.)

If you can't afford a regular masseur, there are a few alternative ways of accommodating your body's need for massage. One is to follow a committed stretching programme; another is to carry out self-massage.

Self-massage

Self-massage has a lot of pluses going for it: it's free, convenient and you can regulate the amount of massage you need.

Obviously the technique of self-massage will be different to the treatment you'd get from a qualified masseur. For a start, most riders won't be professionally trained. And you won't be able to manipulate the same position as would a masseur.

- Before beginning self-massage, it is important to be seated, with your back well supported — against a wall, for example.

- Now bend your knees and massage the calf muscles. Feeling the contours of the muscles, this should be a consistent and firm movement going from the ankle to the back of the knee.

- Continue the massage along the hamstring, up the back of the thigh and round to the quadriceps in front, with the movement always being towards the torso rather than away from it.

- The thigh can be massaged further, with a firmer rub of the muscle — again, always towards the torso.

- Shake the mass of the quadriceps around the bone, before finishing up with a last, lighter rub.

■ Embrocations

84

Another important element in both given and self-massage is the use of embrocations, or massage creams. The cheapest one to use is baby oil. Qualified, experienced masseurs often use more sophisticated (and expensive) creams which have varying effects.

Some embrocations are only used before a race or when training in cold weather. These can come in mild, medium and hot treatments. With all forms, though, only a light rub is needed. It is designed to provide a mild warmth and protection from the cold, rather than the deep massage you need after a race. But be warned — if embrocations are massaged too deep, the burning sensation they create can be almost unbearable.

The cream you use should be petroleum-based as this is water-resistant. Unfortunately, this means it is difficult to wash off after riding. A cologne or spirit-based substance is the best method for removing it. If the skin is still burning annoyingly, an ideal way to soothe the pain is to rub a sliced lemon on the affected skin.

The key joints and muscles that need embrocations are the knees, calf-muscles and thighs. Some riders also use creams on their lower backs.

Stretching

There is a feast of possible stretching exercises for cyclists. Below is one example of a stretching routine. It is recommended that at least 20 minutes is spent on one circuit of these exercises.

It's not vital to have a personal assistant, but it is recommended that a qualified trainer explains the benefits and risks of various stretching exercises before any programme is undertaken.

Stretching is imperative to any cyclist's training regime. An ideal time of day to tackle a stretching programme is first thing in the morning.

MUSCLE GROUPS ....

lumbar region

gluteal region

hip extension

hip flexion

hamstring region

quadriceps region

knee flexion

tibia region

calf region

knee extension

ankle flexion

ankle extension

STRETCHING
ROUTINE ·

A 20-minute circuit of these exercises is recommended

Shoulder Stretch

- Standing with your feet slightly apart, extend the arms and interlock the fingers so the palms are facing outwards.
- Raise your arms above you while keeping your back straight. You should feel the shoulders and pectoral muscles stretching.
- Repeat, but this time with your arms behind you. You'll have to work harder because, if your back is straight, you'll naturally have less flexibility than when you raised your arms in front of you.

Lateral Stretch

- Again standing with feet slightly apart, yet with the knees slightly bent this time and arms at your sides, raise one arm above your head while the other stays at your side.
- As your raised arm goes higher, let the arm by your side slide down your leg. You will feel the muscles in your raised arm stretching. To gain maximum benefit don't let your head drop or body tip forward.
- After feeling one side stretch, repeat the exercise, but with the other arm raised; if there is any pain felt, however, don't continue.

Quadriceps Stretch

- Stand up straight — preferably near a wall or chair for balance.
- Lift one foot up behind you. Hold the ankle to keep the position.
- Simultaneously allow the back to arch. The stretch should be felt in the thigh muscle of the bent leg.
- Repeat the exercise with the other leg.

Calf-muscle Stretch

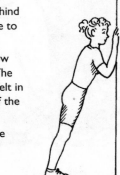

- Stand 1 metre (about 3 feet) from a wall. Keep both feet and heels flat on the ground, with toes pointing towards the wall.
- Put your hands on the wall, keeping the torso and hips straight.
- While bending your elbows, allow your shoulders to slowly move closer to the wall as if your were doing a push-up in reverse.
- Once you feel the calf muscles stretching, hold the position for 30 seconds.

Hamstring Stretch

- Position the feet so they are slightly wider apart than your shoulder width.
- Bend over and take hold of an ankle, while allowing both knees to bend slightly.
- Slowly try and straighten the leg which you are holding until the hamstring can be felt stretching.
- Meanwhile, make sure the other knee is always bent during the exercise.
- Hold the stretch position for 30 seconds and then repeat it on the other side.

Abductor Stretch

- Position one foot outwards so the inside thigh is stretched.
- Then gradually bend the other knee to increase the stretch.
- After 30 seconds or so, straighten the knee to finish the exercise.
- Repeat on the other side.

Lumbar and Hip Stretch

- Lying on the floor with your knees bent, raise one knee towards the chest and hold it until the stretch sensation is felt.
- As with all exercises, don't overdo it if it hurts.
- After holding the position, release the knee and slowly let the foot back down on the floor.
- Repeat with the other leg.

Gluteal Stretch

- Lie on your back with your knees slightly bent.
- Lift the ankle of one leg up and put it on the knee of the other leg.
- Grasp the thigh of the leg on which your ankle is placed with both hands and draw it in towards your chest. This should bring the supporting leg in towards you as well, simultaneously stretching the buttock of the other leg.
- Hold this position and then release slowly. Repeat the action using the other leg.

Not only does it help stimulate body and mind for a new day, but it is also a facet of physical training which helps heighten flexibility without requiring an excess load of energy.

Stretching should be undertaken both before and after training or racing. This helps to keep the muscles agile, diminishes the risk of injury or strain and improves blood flow throughout the system. Should a rider begin a training session or race without stretching, there is always the possibility of cramps or muscle strain.

Stretching exercise should aim at increasing flexibility by increasing the length of muscles with a deliberate yet controlled force. It is a simple and safe procedure, providing certain rules and principles are followed. These are:

- Don't overdo any stretching exercise. The aim is not to stretch so it hurts, but until the exercise provides the sensation of the muscle being gently exerted. When that point is reached, hold it for 30–60 seconds.

- In between exercises, concentrate on what the exercise you've just completed has achieved and what part of the body being affected. Concentrate just as much on being relaxed too.

- Carry out stretching exercises on a particular muscle which is tight several times in the day.

- Always maintain a stretching programme during any period of recovery from injury. It is OK to stretch that area once pain from the injury has dissipated, but don't over-stress the area which has been injured.

- Flexibility does not come overnight. It is dependent on regular exercise. So the more stretching exercises you do, the more flexibility will be achieved.

- Never aim to achieve a level of flexibility which is beyond your ability. Everyone has varying levels of prowess — concentrate on your own potential and don't be tempted to compare yourself to others.

Ergogenic Aids

Ergogenic aids are performance-improving devices which have physical and psychological influences. They include ergometers, warm-up exercises, music, visualisation, hypnosis, vitamins, nutritional substances, oxygen and drugs.

The last aid — drugs — is one which MUST be ignored. Not only will you be cheating if you use drugs, but they can also do you irreparable damage. (*See Appendix on page 207 for the UCI's list of banned and restricted drugs.*) Steroids are commonly used for increasing muscle bulk, even though they can have powerful side effects. A less harmful way to increase muscle mass is with weights, which also help strengthen bones, tendons and ligaments, etc.

Another important ergogenic aid is vitamin supplements (*see below*). Some people are sceptical about their benefit but, in our opinion, any cyclist on a rigorous training regime will need more than the vitamins in their diet.

Ergogenic aids help to provide variety in a training regime as well. You should try out different aids and see what suits you best. However, don't use an ergogenic aid in competition without having tested it before in training.

Vitamin Supplements

Vitamins come from fresh foods and can be taken as a supplement in tablet form.

Whole foods — those without additives — are the best foods to eat. Another way to ensure you get the maximum intake of vitamins from fresh foods is to eat them raw whenever possible. Cooking kills vitamins.

A well-balanced diet should provide an adequate supply of vitamins for beginner cyclists. It is when your goals and training patterns increase — and therefore the demands on the body too — that extra sources of vitamins are called for.

Vitamin supplements in tablet form should be used on the advice of a doctor. Vitamins A, D, E and K are fat-soluble and therefore will not pass through the system when taken excessively. Vitamins B and C are water-soluble and therefore can escape the body through urine when taken in excess.

Basic **First Aid**

There is a never-ending list of possible injuries a cyclist can experience. The most common include: colds, bronchitis, cramps, saddle sores, hyperventilation, tendinitis, cuts and broken bones.

Always consult a doctor when necessary. However, there are certain things you can do to alleviate the health problems associated with cycling.

Colds should be treated immediately, otherwise they can lead to severe illnesses which could threaten your entire season. Certainly, when you have a cold don't commit the greatest sin of them all — to keep on training with the belief that you can sweat it out.

If you have a cold the first remedy is to keep warm, stay indoors, rest and take plenty of fluids regularly. Aspirin is also an effective substance to take, starting with two

The RICE Theory

This theory doesn't suggest you eat rice for your injuries! It's an easy-to-remember acronym for a pattern of immediate treatment after a crash. It may well heal a minor injury or at least minimise the chances of a serious injury worsening before you're able to see a doctor.

- **R**

  stands for rest. Lie down if you can. Try to make yourself as comfortable as possible and stay warm.

- **I**

  stands for ice which should be applied with an ice pack. It will make damaged blood vessels contract and therefore slow down any bleeding and minimise the chances of bruising. Do not apply heat to any injury for at least 48 hours, as it will only maximise the dangers of bruising and swelling.

- **C**

  stands for compression. This is done by dressing the wounded area with a pressure bandage. It will minimise the swelling. The bandage should be taken off before you go to sleep at night.

- **E**

  stands for elevation. The injured part of the body should be raised above the level of your heart. This will help excess fluids drain away and therefore minimise swelling.

soluble tablets every four hours — although don't take more than eight in a day. A vitamin C supplement is often found in aspirin, but if it isn't, then a dose of 1 gram of vitamin C every four hours in an effervescent form in between the aspirin doses will be helpful. This procedure should kill a cold within 48 hours, if not quicker. If your cold lasts up to a week, then you should see your doctor.

Bronchitis is an illness cyclists are particularly vulnerable to because of the fact that they cycle in all types of weather. If it hits you, stay indoors and rest. It is also advisable to see a doctor. However, in its early stages, bronchitis can be treated by special inhalation treatments. These require the mixing of herbal balms with hot water of which the vapours, when inhaled, will help eliminate the bronchial bug.

Coughs and sore throats are common symptoms of colds and bronchitis and these can be treated by over-the-counter remedies. However, be careful not to buy one which contains substances which are on the UCI's list of banned and restricted drugs (*see Appendix on page 207*). The slightest negligence of this advice could find you rating positive in a dope test.

Other basic remedies for coughs and sore throats range from taking aspirin and vitamin C to drinking hot water mixed with honey, lemon and glycerin, which should be available in most chemists.

Infections, while they are an ever-present danger, are ailments which can be avoided by prevention. The odds of infection are always minimised if you maintain strict hygiene in nutrition, clothing and general personal care.

In the event of infection occurring, there are certain measures you can take. For example, saddle sores can be avoided or minimised by ensuring you have a high-quality chamois inserted in your cycling shorts, and by washing them regularly. Furthermore, before riding you should lubricate the chamois with special creams which are available in chemists or cycle shops. These creams minimise friction between the saddle and the perineum.

If you do get a saddle sore, treat the infected area with an antiseptic cream and rest. If you must race, or are in the middle of a stage race, there are special anaesthetic and antiseptic creams which a race/team doctor could provide.

Do not train if the sore has developed into a boil (these can arise in other parts of the body as well). And make sure the area is washed several times a day, or as much as possible if you must race. Certainly don't allow anyone but a doctor to lance or try to squeeze the pus out of a boil.

For other ailments, here are a few suggested remedies:

- Cramps can be treated by stretching the tightened muscle the opposite way to which it is contracted and pressing your thumb into the thickest part of the muscle until the knot dissipates. Or you could use a cold spray (most race doctors should have this).

- Cuts and grazes should be cleaned with antiseptic or soap and water and covered with sterile dressings.

- Blisters should be cleaned and compressed with a cool pressing to minimise inflammation. When draining blisters, make sure the needle is sterile, wash the affected area properly and cover with a sterile dressing.

- Sunburn and insect bites should be treated as soon as possible with antiseptic creams, which will ease swelling and lessen chances of infection.

Other ailments like tendonitis, sprains and strains can be treated with the RICE theory.

For many infections, a doctor will prescribe antibiotics. It is important that when riders are on a course of antibiotics they follow the full course as prescribed, even if the infection apparently disappears before it is completed. Antibiotics can have side effects with other supplements and foodstuffs which will need respective limitation during an antibiotics programme. For example, iron or mineral supplements should not be taken during an antibiotic course. Antibiotics will attack both natural beneficial and harmful bacteria, but an increased vitamin C intake and consumption of natural yoghurt will help to minimise this.

5 Physiology and Psychology

Physiology and psychology are two major ingredients in racing. Everyone has varying levels of strengths and weaknesses in both departments. While there are certainly born champions — people who possess great physical advantages — there are also many cyclists who have become winners because of their mental prowess.

Physiology

What Type of Cyclist are You?

There are physical limits to what type of cyclist you can be. Some riders are better suited as sprinters, while others make great time-triallists, stage racers or even climbers. However, this is an equation very much dependent on the heart *and* muscle make-up in the body. There aren't any set rules and although there are similarities in body types among the different disciplines, there are also exceptions.

Most sprinters tend to have stockier upper and lower bodies which equip them for the sudden bursts and push-and-shove accelerations of mass sprints. And pure climbers — that is, those riders who excel in the mountains — often have skinny torsos and almost spindly legs. Their physique — while often leaving them susceptible to being dropped on the flat where they have little resistance to winds (unlike bigger riders) — is perfect for the mountains, where their power-to-weight ratio is superior to other riders.

Mental prowess: a quality which has helped Dean Woods get to where he is today.

92

Then there are those riders who are tall, strong and heavy and who may not have the agility to sprint or climb. They can be valuable as either time-triallists, team riders or 'domestiques' where sheer strength is necessary for chasing attacks, for riding in front of their leader to protect him/her from energy-sapping winds and to lead him or her out for the sprints or attacks.

The best all-rounders, like those who win races such as the Tour de France, are usually born with a valuable combination of strength and nimbleness which suits them in every domain — on the flat, in time trials and in the mountains. Such are the rare qualities of a Tour champion — and the reason why only a very few can win.

Whether a cyclist is a natural sprinter or someone suited for longer endurance events depends on the ratio of slow and fast-twitch muscle fibres. Muscles are an amalgamation of long fibres made of cells. They are located in the body in pairs. Each muscle which produces one motion with a pulling effect has a 'twin' which produces the opposite motion. So, for any movement to be made, one muscle must contract while the other relaxes. There are two types of muscle fibres in the body — fast and slow-twitch.

Fast-twitch Muscle Fibres

These are more suited for high-speed, short-duration anaerobic exertions like sprinting. Sprint cyclists have a greater ratio of fast-twitch muscle fibres to slow-twitch ones. They are fuelled on glucose, which produces a high degree of lactic acid build-up in a sprint, giving pain.

94 MUSCLE FIBRES

**Biochemical characteristics
of fast and slow-twitch muscle fibres**

	Fast	Slow
Glycogen content	high	low
Glycotic enzyme levels	high	low
Contraction speed	high	low
Endurance level	low	high
Capillary density	low	high
Oxidative enzyme levels	low	high
Fat content	low	high
Myoglobin content	low	high

▪ Slow-twitch Muscle Fibres

There is less power and speed in slow-twitch muscle fibres. However, they are capable of greater endurance.

They also use oxygen more efficiently. So the greater the efficiency of oxygen use, the more fuel is burned and so there will be less build-up of lactic acid. Slow-twitch actions may increase the production of carbon dioxide, but such a waste product is less painful than lactic waste (*see chart opposite*).

The Three Energy Systems

Muscle contraction is the process which creates movement. To attain and keep it, energy is needed. Energy is provided by the breakdown of a substance called adenosine triphosphate (ATP), of which there are three main sources:

I. Anaerobic Alactic ATP: the first 10-second energy system

It is from this system that a cyclist gets the burst of energy necessary for high-speed or high-resistance actions; these can extend from 1 to 10 seconds. Examples of this include standing starts, sprints or sudden accelerations to attack or chase a break.

As with any form of activity, a warm-up is required beforehand to ensure that muscles are loose and not tight and therefore susceptible to injury. A warm-up also gets the blood going and the flow of oxygen moving. However, this energy system does not rely only on energy, but also on the stored energy supply of ATP.

2. Anaerobic Lactic Acid: the 10 seconds to 2 minutes speed endurance energy system

This system is another anaerobic pathway (i.e. a system not requiring oxygen). At later stages when there is not enough oxygen for the aerobic system, it is a system which contributes to performance.

The system relies on carbohydrate fuel and is the source of lactic acid. It is a system more associated with fast than with slow-twitch muscle fibres and supplies energy for hard efforts of between 10 seconds to 2 minutes.

The presence of lactic acid is what makes a rider's legs feel swollen and heavy. It also slows you down the more it builds up. You can develop your tolerance to lactic acid, although this requires much training at periods where this system is used.

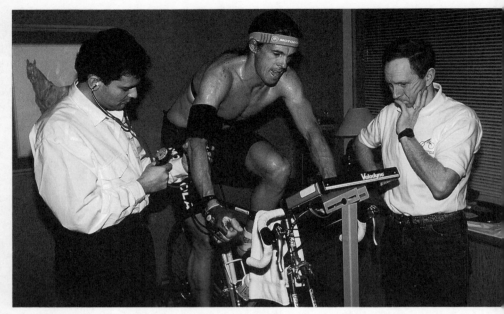

Australian Phil Anderson undergoes physiological testing under the eyes of Motorola team doctor, Massimo Testa (left), and his personal trainer, Ludwig van de Putte (right).

96

3. Aerobic:
the endurance oxygen energy system

This is a system reliant on oxygen which feeds off carbohydrate and fat. The heart and lungs are vital in this system as it is through them that the blood carrying oxygen passes en route to fuelling the muscle cells.

You would use this system in efforts lasting from 30 seconds onwards, as well as in the recovery process after an effort.

It's also a system which can be developed. A minimum of 30 minutes of high-intensity exercise is needed to improve the muscle's energy production capacity and the oxygen delivery system.

The following chart provides a graphic explanation of the conversion time between these three energy systems during a workout.

There are two key moments in the energy shift: after 10 seconds the anaerobic alactic system shifts much of its energy demands to the anaerobic lactic system; after 2 minutes the demands shift heavily from the lactic anaerobic system to the aerobic system.

**Approximate per cent contributions
of energy systems**

Work Time Maximal Effort	Alactic Anaerobic	Lactic Anaerobic	Aerobic
5 sec	85	10	5
10 sec	50	35	15
30 sec	15	65	20
1 min	8	62	30
2 min	4	46	50
4 min	2	28	70
10 min	1	9	90
30 min	negligible	5	95
1 hour	negligible	2	98
2 hours	negligible	1	99

The Vital Capacities

The three key elements of the respiratory system are the lungs, heart and blood.

Training programmes rely heavily on the efficient functioning of these capacities. Respiratory and cardiovascular levels improve when the bloodstream can better move its nutrients to the lungs and heart.

The **lungs** diffuse oxygen taken from inhaled air to the blood. They expel carbon dioxide when you exhale.

The measurement of efficient oxygen supply to the muscles is called VO_2 max. It is measured in millilitres of oxygen per minute per kilogram of body weight (or cubic inches of oxygen per minute per pound) and is the rate at which oxygen is used by the body during peak efforts. Maximum effort in training will increase a rider's VO_2 max. level.

Vital capacity — the volume of air which passes through the lungs during maximum inhalation and exhalation — can only be marginally conditioned through training. However, the greatest advantage of training here is that it enables you to make efficient use of your existing capacity.

An average healthy adult during rest may inhale between 6 to 8 litres (366 to 488 cubic inches) of air per minute, from which 0.3 litres (18.3 cubic inches) of oxygen may be extracted. A fit cyclist can inhale between 120 to 180 litres

(7323 to 10 984 cubic inches) of air per minute, taking in more than 5 litres (305 cubic inches) of oxygen from the effort.

The **heart** transports blood into the system and boosts the cyclist's fuel supply. The bigger the heart, the better.

Cardiac output is the amount of blood pushed out of the heart and into the system in a set period of time. It is measured in litres (or cubic inches) per minute.

Training has a great effect on heart rates. Well-conditioned cyclists generally have lower pulse rates when resting. And they have higher stroke volumes — that is, the amount of blood transported into the system per heart beat.

Long-distance training helps condition the heart, while interval work helps the heart to adapt to maximum stroke volume.

It's worth remembering, though, that the heart can only pump what blood it has. Hence the muscles, when contracted and relaxed alternately, act as a pumping system to send blood back into the heart. When cycling, you should pay attention to muscle relaxation and contraction.

The **blood** is a common link between many components in the body and it provides two key services: firstly, it delivers oxygen, glucose and other nutrients to the system and removes carbon dioxide and lactic acid for either reconstruction or disposal from the body; secondly, blood helps to avert chemical changes in the tissues when acid wastes are produced by metabolic activity.

However, blood itself undergoes several changes during heavy training. There are increases in volume of the amount pumped by the heart each minute and in haemoglobin which exists in red blood cells carrying the oxygen. And blood can also undergo flow changes from unused muscles to active ones.

Developing the Three Systems

The best way to develop the three systems is with interval training. This is a series of hard efforts of varying duration, interspersed with rest or recovery periods. These spells can be specifically designed to develop one or more of the systems.

During a recovery spell, the depleted supply of ATP is replenished by the aerobic system. A proportion of oxygen debt is restored and this means that ATP will be available again as an energy source for the next hard effort. This also means that the lactic acid system will be less taxed than if a rider were to tackle a continuous effort with no relief. The price to pay is that the intensity of work can be greater.

Nobody is the Same

No cyclist is the same. Age, sex, energy capacity, strength, style and psychological levels all vary, but what makes cyclists truly different from each other is their capacity to meet training demands.

■ Age

The element of age is an important factor. Age group competition has grown rapidly in recent years with limits in both youth and veteran categories expanding.

These are the questions to consider when you're planning a training or racing programme:

- To what extent is competition harmful mentally and physically to youngsters and older veterans?
- Are long rides risky for young and old cyclists?
- In what way should old and young cyclists plan for competition?

A key to the above is to make sure a juvenile or veteran has been given medical approval to compete. They should also have an experienced trainer or coach working with them to nurture their skills and develop progressive training regimes. And the chosen goals need to be achievable and realistic for each age group.

In most cases, younger and older cyclists are able to adapt to the training regimes of mature cyclists. Everyone can reach their maximum physical potential, although you need to understand that everyone has varying levels of inherited abilities.

▮ Biological Development

An important factor in a youngster's cycling career hinges on the difference between their biological and chronological ages — that is, the difference between their level of functional ability compared to their actual age. For example, it is not uncommon to see a 14-year-old with the physical ability of a 16-year-old. However, it's worth remembering that if a young rider is an early developer with limited ability, they will often lose the advantage they have when their chronological age reaches their biological age. Many junior and juvenile champions fall into this category.

The challenge facing early developers is to confront equal competition when they get older. Their initial successes are often a result of biological advantages and not just hard training, as will necessarily be the case when they are older. Hence, while some are labelled future champions, the very same riders may retire early when the challenges become too great.

It is generally accepted that the functions of a person's physical make-up will improve or develop until maturity. There is then a plateau of ability before the aging process inevitably chips away ones level of skill. Increased physical activity such as cycling does slow down the process. What does vary is the age at which maturity arrives. For **agility,** 12 is the age when this is at its peak. There is a slight amount of development until 14, but at a much diminished rate.

Strength is a factor which depends on body weight. However, its level generally reaches 80% of an adult's maximum at 16 years of age for males and 14 years for females. Peak strength is usually reached at 20 for females and 20 to 30 for males. Thereafter, as long as physical activity is regular, the muscle mass you have will stay with you through the middle years before degenerating after approximately 45 years of age.

A sensitive issue with strength development in youngsters is the use of weights. For a long time weights were discouraged for fear they would injure and hinder the natural growth process. While some animal studies have reportedly shown that heavy resistance exercise can help development, the effects on youngsters have not yet been accurately measured.

So have a cautious and conservative outlook on this aspect of training until proper research has been carried out. Certainly, heavy weight-training should not be carried out before puberty. And, at the other end of the age spectrum, older people should avoid isometric exercises because they increase blood pressure.

Power is something one attains very quickly. Yet it hinges greatly on the natural **speed** a cyclist has too. This latter element is affected by the central nervous system which reaches peak development at 14 years of age. Once again, the age process slows down speed, although active people will lose their speeds more slowly than non-active people. It has even been suggested that the aging process itself can be slowed down in people who keep their nerve cells as active as possible — one reason to keep active throughout your life!

The crucial age for deciding on whether or not to focus on sports like cycling which require reaction speed and movement frequency is 14. And in cycling, a good indicator of one's potential is pedalling speed. Regular testing of pedalling speed should be carried out up to the ages of 16 and 17.

◼ Women

Female responses to training are more or less the same as those of a male's. This is because cellular mechanisms influencing the physiological and biological responses to cycling are the same in both sexes.

Yet there are some significant differences in male/female make-up which influence respective performances:

Body-size composition: compared to an adult male, a female of the same age is approximately 7 to 10 centimetres (2¾ to 4 inches) shorter, 11 to 13 kilograms (24 to 29 pounds) lighter, has an average 25% body-fat reading (compared to 7% to 15% in males) and has 18 to 20 kilograms (40 to 44 pounds) less fat-free weight.

Energy systems: most research in this area has been on the aerobic system. With the anaerobic alactic system, the muscular concentration of ATP is the same per unit of muscle. Yet anaerobic lactic systems differ. After an all-out effort a woman's build-up of lactic acid is generally lower than a male's, which indicates that she is using her oxygen system more efficiently. As for the aerobic system, while the differences are minimal in

youth, they become pronounced between 20 and 30 years of age when body sizes and compositions are vastly different.

Generally, a woman's VO$_2$ max. is smaller than a man's. That's because women usually have smaller heart and blood volumes and less haemoglobin than men.

For example, tests in swimming where male and female weight differences are reduced by the buoyancy from water have shown that a female's endurance is much closer to a male's. Yet in cycling, where body weight determines the degree of work and effort, a woman's VO$_2$ max. will be far less because she has greater natural body-fat levels and therefore an extra load to carry.

Muscle strength: a woman's is approximately two-thirds of a man's, although the degree of difference varies between upper and lower bodies. There is less strength difference in the legs than in the arms. Leg strength is actually the same when compared to body sizes in women and men. And when compared to lean body weight, female leg strength is even greater. Studies have even revealed that strength — when compared to muscle size — is equal for both sexes. However, as males have larger muscle groups than females, the actual force released by males is greater.

With weight training a female can make increases in strength by up to 44%, although as women have lower testosterone levels than men, their already diminished muscle mass (compared to that of a man) should not increase.

Providing women follow a controlled and well-supervised programme, the significant changes they should experience are:

- minimal change in body weight;
- marked loss of relative and absolute body fat;
- gain in lean body weight.

Menstruation: for female cyclists the menstrual cycle can lead to irritability, anxiety and bouts of mental depression which can affect performance.

Studies have shown that some cyclists experienced poorer standards of competition and training just before and during menstruation. Many of these were cyclists in endurance events. The best results, on the other hand, were recorded up to 15 days after a period.

This can lead to two conclusions:

- it is better to undertake heavy training after the menstrual cycle;
- wherever possible, the post-menstrual cycle should correspond with a major competition date.

It is recommended, however, that you see a qualified doctor to discuss your particular needs with regard to competition and training.

Psychology

A cyclist may have all the equipment, back-up support and be incredibly fit, but without the right psychological balance, he or she won't get very far.

There are three key components to achieving this balance — goal-setting, self-confidence and overcoming competitive anxiety.

Goal-setting

Having a goal is the key to any cyclist's motivation, whether it is to win a world title, a national championship, to finish a randonnée or simply to have a good time. Without goals we would not have the urge to mount a bicycle and pedal.

However, what must not be ignored is the need to set *achievable* goals. It is better to set a goal, reach it and then progress to another one than to fail in the enterprise. Unrealistic goals can lead to disappointment, frustration and a loss of self-respect and confidence.

This might sound like a basic and obvious principle to follow but, rest assured, sport is full of cautionary tales of people who have demanded too much of themselves too soon.

There are certain guidelines to follow when setting a goal. Make sure your goals are:

- achievable;
- prioritised so that there are no clashes with other aspects of your life;
- a way of improving performance;
- measurable;
- made with a view to your long-term ambitions and current sporting, personal and professional circumstances;
- made with the competition and challenges facing you so the final result can be used as a performance reference;
- accepted by all parties concerned — yourself, your coach, your team.

Providing you've been conscientious in training, a training log will also act as a handy morale-boosting tool prior to an event. By taking a regular look back at goals which have been achieved — day-to-day and week-to-week — a cyclist will feel the sense of confidence which comes from well-organised preparation. Ideally, the motivation to do justice to the preparation with a good performance will result.

Self-confidence

Your opinion of yourself — your self-image — is created through everyday experience and is influenced by the opinions of those around you — your coach, parents, fellow cyclists, etc. Self-confidence can grow with maturity, but a way of speeding up the process is to develop your powers of positive thinking.

Positive Thinking

Everyone loves to win, but the greatest challenge may be to come to terms with losing. This may be disappointing, but there is a positive side to any loss. Foremost is that you can learn from your mistakes and improve the next time. If that occurs, your satisfaction will be even greater.

Another element to building self-confidence is the ability to be flexible in your thinking. You may have to cope with circumstances beyond your control. These can include punctures and other mechanical malfunctions, a crash caused by sudden gusts of winds, spilled diesel on the road or dangerous bike handling by another rider.

Even these examples of bad luck can be confronted positively. Instead of giving up, make a quick mental assessment of what has happened. You may have to redefine your goals, but at least you have a positive challenge to tackle rather than taking a defeatist way out.

Overcoming Competitive Anxiety

Most people feel fear, apprehension and tension in a competitive environment. Different people react differently to stress. You can either fight it or let it beat you. Positive thinking should help to combat anxiety, but you should also be aware of an all-too-common element in sport — psychological sabotage. Here, too, there are techniques you can use to overcome the anxiety it causes.

Psychological Sabotage

The aim of this 'mind game' is for a cyclist to psychologically unsettle a rival before competition. This might come in the form of apparently innocent remarks about personal appearance or equipment which can instill last-minute self-doubt. Or it could be attention-seeking body language which may distract the person's mental focus on the coming event.

The best way to tackle this form of sabotage is to develop a knack of anticipation. Learn to identify such actions and words for what they are. Come the day of a major competition, you should be at the peak of your training and confident and strong enough to be able to fend off such psychological attacks.

◼ Visualisation

This is another measure which will fortify your defence before a race. It will give you greater self-assurance and help to 'psych' you up.

By running the coming event — or its crucial parts — through your mind beforehand, your subconscious will be activated to react instinctively when the actual moment arrives. Naturally, you should visualise the race positively. Try to imagine making a winning break or sprint and climbing or descending with graceful speed in the company of the best in the pack.

Like all aspects of cycling — or any sport — visualisation requires time to develop its effectiveness. If you've never tried it, you may find yourself put off by the ego-boosting involved. However, try to recognise its purpose, which is as a form of mental rehearsal of the coming event and a buffer to the threat of psychological needling.

Mexican Angel Arroyo (second from right) sees his self-confidence take a shake in this tricky descent in the 1990 Kellogg's Tour of Britain.

6 Training

To achieve the most out of bicycle and body, a training regime suited to individual goals, ability and lifestyle is a must. Having said that, however, outlining a *proper* training regime is not a matter of saying you will ride — for example — four days a week. There is a thorough process of preparation and training on and off the bike to go through. And to best implement it, you should have a basic understanding of how the body works during this period (*see also chapters 4 and 5*).

This chapter will tell you how to get the best out of what cycling has to offer

The **Biomechanics** **of** Cycling

Biomechanists are forever developing methods of maximising sports skills by studying and correcting the athlete's motion and the forces behind it. This study can help determine which factors are helping or hindering an athlete to perform.

Basically, force is what changes a body from a state of rest to that of motion. A unit of force is the level of acceleration produced when a force acts on 1 kilogram (2 pounds) of weight. This unit is called a newton and it is the force required to move a 1-kilogram (2-pound) mass at 1 metre (1 yard) per second.

Pedal Action

The most basic movement of cycling is the pedal action. Yet it can be the most misunderstood and badly practised.

▮ Muscles and Joints

The muscles used in cycling exist around several key joints — the thigh, knee and foot. And it is the combined force around each joint which produces the maximum result, or output, of power, speed and acceleration.

When several joints are called upon, it is vital that the sequence and timing of your movement is correct. For example, joints with large muscle groups should be used before those with small muscle groups which are located at the end of limbs.

Australian rider Allan Peiper
was a stickler for following
his training regime to the
letter before retiring
after the 1992
season.

The Three Main Forces

1 **GRAVITATIONAL** force is what pulls any mass towards the ground. Yet force of gravity is the degree of that force which acts on a mass and in turn enables it to release an equal force on its support. That force on the support is body weight.

2 **CENTRIPETAL** force is the force which enables a body or mass to move in a circle and is directed towards the centre. An example is the pull in a string attached to a mass when it is swung around. That force varies according to mass, speed and radius.

3 **REACTIONARY** forces are opposite forces to those which act on a body. To every action there is an equal and opposite reaction. For example, in cycling, whenever a force acts on a body, there is always some reactionary or opposite force on another part of the body.

These include work, power, resistance and friction:

Work in biomechanics means the result of force producing motion. It is gauged by the distance moved in the application of a force in its direction.

$$Work = Force \times Distance\ moved\ in\ direction\ of\ force$$

Power is the rate at which work is done.

$$Power = \frac{Work}{Time}$$

Resistance is what creates an impeding or stopping effect.

Friction is the force which opposes the slipping motion of two forces when in contact with each other. (This measurement depends on the material of the two surfaces, as some combinations create varying degrees of friction.)

The muscle groups are divided into the following: hip flexors and extendors, knee flexors and extendors and ankle flexors and extendors (*see illustration on page 85*).

Pedal action involves pushing and pulling. As one leg pushes down on the pedal from the 12-o'clock to 6-o'clock position, the other is pulling up. In between the push and pull actions there is also a drag action. The entire arc motion incorporates various muscles at different times.

Applied Forces

Maximum force varies, depending on whether you are seated or standing up and out of the saddle.

When on the saddle, force reaches its peak when the pedal motion is between 60 and 90 degrees on the push action. Minimum force occurs at 300 degrees, or when the pull action is nearing its end.

When out of the saddle the theory is similar, but applied forces undergo a rotational movement of 30 degrees as the rider is positioned far more forward and over the handlebars.

Fluidity is the key to efficient movement. A cyclist should strive for smoothness in the pedal action. So the transfer of use from larger to smaller muscle groups should be unbroken. A fluid action will enhance your performance where a broken or uneven action will hinder it. There are several key signs to look for when your action is not correct or fluid enough:

- when your knee/s is/are thrown outwards when pedalling;
- when there is too much lateral movement of the cycle when you are off the saddle;
- when your off-the-saddle starting technique appears cramped and unstylish;
- when you use too many energy-wasting body movements in your cycling.

Such directional problems generally result from strength imbalances or poor technique. When you identify the problem, the exact area of the pedal action needs to be pinpointed and corrected.

Resistant Forces

The four main forces resisting pedal flow are gravity, friction, rolling and drag:

Gravity doesn't really come into force until a rider climbs. There are three variables to minimising its impact — you can reduce body weight, bicycle weight or both.

Bicycle weights vary from between 7 to 11 kilograms (15 to 24 pounds). While weight reduction here can be a help, never attempt to sacrifice rigidity in the bicycle. It's better to lose a kilogram (about 2 pounds) of body weight than a kilogram of bicycle equipment.

Phil Anderson, out of the saddle, in a time trial during the 1991 Tour de France.

Body weight is arguably the aspect a cyclist should attend to first. Gravity doesn't discriminate between body or bicycle weight, but less body weight is a more controllable variable in creating a more efficient person–bike force.

The success of each technique can be judged if we compare two weight-loss strategies:

- In the first, if a rider drills 30 holes in the chain-wheel, the bike may be 14 grams (½ ounce) lighter. That can lead to an increase of 0.002 kph (0.001 mph) on a 10% gradient hill, or a distance of 3 kilometres (1.86 miles) in a hour's ride.

- In the second, a rider with a body weight of 75 kilograms (165 pounds) and 7% excess body fat may be carrying 5 kilograms (11 pounds) in excess body weight. Losing this will bear a far greater impact on speed than will the loss of 14 grams off the rider's bike.

The ideal scenario is to have a light and responsive bicycle with a rider at optimal body weight.

Friction has little serious impact on a bicycle which is finely tuned (which we will assume it is in your case).

Rolling resistance is an influential factor in impeding fluid pedal flow. Rolling resistance means the point of contact between the machine and its surface, so tyre pressure is important. Research has shown that rolling resistance can increase from 10.34 to 12.5% when tyre pressure is lowered from 105 to 85 psi.

Obviously, road surfaces can affect resistance. Automobile research has discovered that by going from concrete to bitumen surfaces, resistance can increase by 5%. However, road surfaces aren't an element cyclists can always choose, especially in racing.

Wheel diameter is also a factor to consider when trying to reduce rolling resistance. The smaller the diameter, the greater the resistance, and vice versa. And the rigidity of rims and spoke tension contribute to effectively lowering this type of resistance.

Of all the resistances to pedal flow, **wind drag** is the strongest. When the speed of a bicycle increases, so too does the aerodynamic resistance which a cyclist has to overcome. This, in turn, can be influenced by the projected frontal area and wind direction.

Projected frontal area is determined by body size, bicycle position and the use of aerodynamic equipment — all factors which can be adjusted by cyclists according to the demands that await them.

Large people will have greater frontal areas and therefore a higher degree of wind resistance. However, some large people may also have a greater muscle mass and thus the resources to fight this resistance. Overweight or out-of-condition riders won't have this advantage and won't realise their full potential. Hence the importance of those early off-season training spins!

Wind can increase or lower the speed of air past the body. It is a factor which is out of our control, though you can gauge expected directions and try to cycle on a route which takes the forecast into consideration.

Riders with a 5-kilometre (3-mile) tail-wind behind them, cycling at 45 kph (28 mph) will see resistance lowered from 356 watts (W) to 254 W. A rider cycling at 5 kph (3 mph) into a head-wind of 5 kph will see the wattage of resistance increase from 356 to 483 W. Ultimately, the effort becomes much harder to hold.

Programmes

As your cycling level progresses, so too will the demands on your body. To help you discover your true potential you need a training programme.

A programme shouldn't be hastily thrown together, however. To gain the real benefit of any training, a programme needs to concentrate on the systematic development of strength, flexibility and the energy systems. This requires careful planning which can take weeks and months — even years!

There are five key components to a training programme: intensity, time, quantity, relief periods and repetitions. The training session examples opposite show how these are used, depending on the type of cyclist you are. They also reveal how limited time can be used to maximum benefit.

Endurance:
for road, time-trial and track-endurance riders

Programme A

Ten-minute stretching to warm-up, followed by 40 kilometres (25 miles) of cycling without rest.

Break down the 40 kilometres in the following way:

• the first	10 km (6 mls) at	1.50 min/km (2.50 min/ml)	= 15 minutes
• the second	10 km at	1.43 min/km (2.38 min/ml)	= 14.30 minutes
• the third	10 km at	1.40 min/km (2.33 min/ml)	= 14.00 minutes
• the fourth	10 km at	1.39 min/km (2.31 min/ml)	= 13.90 minutes
		Total training ride	**= 57.20 minutes**

Programme B

Warm-up ride for 20 minutes, followed by the following intervals separated by 2 minutes of easy pedalling in between:

• five repeats of	5-minute efforts at	50 kph (31 mph)	
• five repeats of	1-minute efforts at	55 kph (34 mph)	
• five repeats of	40-second efforts at	57 kph (35 mph)	
	Total training ride		**= 57.30 minutes**

Speed Endurance:
for road, track-endurance, sprint, kilometre and points racers

- Do ten repetitions of 15-seconds' high-speed pedalling. Separate each burst by 1 minute of easy pedalling.

- After a 10-minute recovery, do ten repetitions of sprints, separated by 1 minute of easy pedalling.

TRAINING

Dean Woods, racing here in a time trial of the 1990 Tour of Spain, has always relied on the systematic development of strength, flexibility and the energy systems.

Macro Systems

This is a cyclic way of training where there are lows and peaks in a regime. The peaks are where demands are higher, the lows where recovery is needed.

Recovery is vital in that it enables the body and mind to replenish its reserves. Were you not to rest, the ultimate result would be a downfall in performance.

However, without demands being made on the body a cyclist will not adapt to a higher level of endurance. The fatigue you feel after a workout is your body's adaptation to the threshold you have just gone through.

As you adapt to a higher level of training, the demands increase, although you should obviously set yourself some time limits. These could be:

- short-term — several days to two weeks;
- medium-term — two weeks to six weeks;
- long-term — one year to four years (this is known as the Olympic cycle).

Ten-point Rule for Training

1 Avoiding overload

An element in any cyclist's training pattern. It is the result of the intense demands of a programme which requires the rider's body to adapt to hard work-levels and the stresses which occur in competition.

2 Specificity

All training programmes need to be focused on development of the muscle groups, energy systems, the variety of motions and the demands of an event.

3 Frequency

Long-term training programmes should be scheduled at least two or three times a week.

4 Progression

The frequency and intensity of training must increase gradually as the cyclist adapts to the work and meets the need for overload.

5 Coping with regression

There is always the possibility of a rider's condition dropping due to injury, illness, a slackening of training standards or even psychological troughs.

Six-day track racers, like Dean Woods, rest between events in a nightly programme in makeshift cabins in the middle of the track.

6 Uniformity

There is no set rule to the level of progression in condition. There are always peaks, but also periods where condition can rest on a plateau. This is when a rider's self-confidence is essential to take him or her on to greater achievement.

7 Resting

Over-training is one of the key dangers to any programme. Making sure you don't neglect vital rest periods in a training regime requires as much self-discipline as fulfilling the workload.

8 Assessment

Every cyclist should monitor their personal performance in a training schedule. Periodic medical tests and regular documentation in a training diary of what you do and how you react are important steps.

9 Goal-setting

Long and short-term goals are part of the training recipe too. Your commitment to a goal will make all the difference to your eventual performance.

10 Maintenance

Training can be adapted to minimise overloading while avoiding any loss of condition.

TRAINING

The Training Week

When planning a training week, it is important to include at least three heavy sessions. Obviously the available time, facilities, your age, ambition and ability should be taken into account.

Still, there are several *principles* to remember when preparing for the week ahead:

- Make sure hard sessions are followed or preceded by easier workouts. Allow for 24 to 48 hours' recovery from high-intensity training sessions.
- Avoid hard training sessions the day before or after a race, although some light training should still be done on these days.
- Follow a cyclic pattern: make sure you have a pattern of low periods and peaks (see *Macro Systems on page 114*).

The Training Year

It is important to break down the year into four blocks as well. They are as follows:

1 Active Rest

This is your off-season when you should recover mentally and physically from the previous season's demands. It should last about four to six weeks. However, it needn't be a period of non-activity. Other alternative sports should be pursued which will help you to maintain a certain fitness level and aid a return to specific training later.

2 Foundation

This period lasts about 10 to 12 weeks and is the time when you should develop a base condition. This means going for longer, yet relatively easy rides to build up basic fitness.

3 Preparation

When the energy systems are all developed. This block lasts approximately four months and incorporates an increasing level of intensity in training.

4 Competition

When a rider discovers if he or she has used the training year to their best advantage. This is the part of the season which really counts. Training is hard, but recovery is equally important here too. Besides fine-tuning your condition, it is also a period where your skills must be honed to their full potential.

Training the Systems

▮ Anaerobic Alactate System

Known as the 'speed system', the ideal way to use this system is with intervals. A training session should be split between maximum bursts or sprints and recovery spells which draw on chemical energy (ATP) which is found in fast and slow-twitch muscle fibres.

Before you begin using this system, it is important that you already have a strong base of aerobic condition. If you do not, you won't have the fitness to recover adequately and therefore complete the programme.

Maximum bursts, known as 'ride time', should be about 10 seconds long and can be done in sets, where the total length of each set is about 1 minute. The total amount of time of these sets should be from 8 to 12 minutes. An 8-minute total, for example, equals 480 seconds or 48 x 10-second bursts, of which six would make up one of eight sets.

The recovery spell is designed to allow a replenishment of ATP and should be about six times longer than the ride time. On average, that would mean about 5 to 10 minutes between sets. If you are still fatigued, allow more time for recovery.

▮ Anaerobic Lactate System

This system requires build-up and build-down periods. The energy you use here fuels efforts of between 10 seconds and 2 minutes. The peak of this energy output is between 30 and 50 seconds.

This exercise is primarily reliant on a rider's fast-twitch muscles. And, as with the other systems, the ideal means of development is exposure to the elements. Once again, intervals are the key with a recipe of ride–rest–ride–rest–ride being the *repetition* pattern used.

Here, though, the ride time should be no less than 10 seconds long and no greater than 2 minutes. And the longer the effort, the less the intensity should be. The sets should be split into blocks of 10 to 15 minute periods, although this is a flexible element as each rider's condition and ability to accomplish the workload will vary.

The ratio of rest to work also varies, depending on ability and condition: the greater the work or ride time, the longer the rest should be. Ratios should generally range from 2:1 to 6:1. However, between each set of 10 to 15 minutes, allow around 10 minutes of recovery time to dissipate the build-up of lactic acid.

■ Aerobic System

This oxygen-based system requires the changing use of muscles and the use of different supporting systems. It is an important exercise for all cyclists. Endurance riders need to develop their aerobic capacity to extend prolonged efforts, while sprinters depend on it for recovery from short and sudden bursts of speed.

There are three forms of training this system — long-distance and interval training and fartlek:

1.   Long-distance Training

Overloading the aerobic system takes longer than the anaerobic system as its purpose is to resist general tiredness. A minimum period of 30 minutes' training is necessary to gain any benefit. The period of a maximum time is more open to question. But for 13-year-olds it is recommended they ride no longer than 2 hours, while 16-year-olds should not extend their training beyond 4 hours.

The two keys to improvement in long-distance training are to increase duration and intensity. Make sure you pursue steady progression in both. Start with short, comfortable rides and use this period to focus on skills.

The intensity of your training can increase as your fitness improves. The objective should be to boost your kilometreage, as well as gradually increasing periods of stress. To gauge stress levels, your heart rate is a good indicator. To calculate your maximum heart rate, it is best to see a sports doctor as he or she will know how to work out the test within the limits of your individual condition and health.

However, if you have a clean bill of health and approval from your doctor, there is a rudimentary way of arriving at a figure yourself. Maximum heart rates vary for each individual. They should be determined when you begin or plan your training routine and after a maximum effort over a set period of time or distance, either on a bike or running.

The most efficient way is to use a heart-rate monitor which measures the increase of your heart rate under stress. If you don't have one, simply carry out your planned workout or effort and record your heart rate as soon as you have finished.

To do this, place a finger on your pulse and count the number of beats for 15 seconds; multiply this figure by four to give your maximum heart rate. You could repeat this effort several times to confirm your maximum, although you should allow some time for recovery or for your heart rate to drop to 120 beats per minute (bpm) before doing it again.

It is recommended that riders between 20 and 30 years of age don't ride below 120 bpm if cardiovascular improvement is the goal. In fact, you will not attain a good level of condition unless you ride at more than 120 bpm — a rate of 150 bpm is an ideal level. However, this obviously depends on your physical condition as well. A medical check-up will determine if such training patterns are suitable or not.

Rule of thumb maximum theoretical HR = (220 − age) = 220 − 20 = 200
Resting HR = 60
Training range = MHR − RestingHR = 200 − 60 = 140
∴ 60% training load = RestingHR + 60% Training range = 60 + $\frac{60}{100}$(140) = 144

To calculate your minimum heart rate to benefit from training, use the following equation:

maximum heart rate (MHR) − resting heart rate (RHR) + age × 0.6 + 60

e.g. where MHR = 220, RHR = 60, age = 20,

$$220 - 60 + 20 \times 0.6 + 60 = 144$$

the minimum heart rate would be 144.

70% training level on 38 yrs
with resting pulse of 48 is :
48 + (.7×((220−38) − 48)) =
141.8

2. Interval Training (on Road and Track)

This is a great way to develop speed endurance. Various procedures and recipes of time blocks are used on an off–on–off–on basis. The range is usually from a 10-second sprint to five minutes, with the rider cycling at a pre-determined target heart rate.

An example of interval sprinting is as follows: a rider might sprint for 15 seconds and then ride slowly until their heart rate drops back down to between 120 and 140 bpm. In this instance the objective is to sprint again before the heart rate drops below 120 bpm.

Top riders can do up to 50 sprints. But the increasing level of fatigue will inevitably diminish the speed a rider will attain after the first few sprints. And in longer efforts, such as a 5-minute interval, speeds will be correspondingly lower.

The best way of using interval training is to set a realistic time for a standard distance and ride it at 80% of your maximum speed from opposite directions each time, using varying gear ratios in varying conditions (e.g. cross and tail-winds).

The following graph provides an approximate overview of what target heart rates riders should have in certain age groups and at various periods during an interval session. However, this too can vary according to a rider's medical status and should be checked by a doctor first.

INTERVAL
SESSIONS ••

Target heart rates

Age	Heart rate in effort	HR between repetitions	HR between sets
under 20	190	150	125
20–29	180	140	120
30–39	170	130	110
40–49	160	120	105
50–59	150	115	100
60–69	140	105	90

••

167 − 45 + $\overset{53}{\cancel{20}}$ × 0.6 + 45 =

The best way of using interval training is to set a realistic time for a standard distance and ride it at 80% of your maximum speed from opposite directions each time, using varying gear ratios in varying conditions (e.g. cross and tail-winds).

The following graph provides an approximate overview of what target heart rates riders should have in certain age groups and at various periods during an interval session. However, this too can vary according to a rider's medical status and should be checked by a doctor first.

3.   Fartlek

'Fartlek' is a Swiss word meaning 'speedplay'. Unlike interval training, fartlek efforts and relief periods are not pre-determined. It is basically a more informal type of interval training and is best suited to road cycling as it relies on a variety of terrain which give many 'natural' challenges to the cyclist. For example, you might sprint to traffic lights as a form of interval work. Hills are of great benefit — long, short or undulating — because they provide variety. The ideal distance for a fartlek effort is about 2 kilometres (1.2 miles) at racing pace, repeated four or five times, or until fatigue sets in.

The following is an example of a fartlek workout:

FARTLEK WORKOUT

Activity	Duration
warm-up ride	15 minutes
increase tempo	6 to 10 minutes
cycle easily	5 minutes
do sprints of between 100 to 150 metres (109 to 164 yards)	until fatigue sets in
cycle easily	10 to 20 minutes
sprint uphill at maximum effort for 100 to 200 metres (109 to 219 yards) with first 50 metres (55 yards) off the saddle only	repeat until fatigue sets in
cycle easily	5 minutes
cycle at increased tempo	2 to 3 minutes
cycle at slightly slower pace	10 minutes

While such fartlek workouts develop all capacities, its one failing is that it lacks the specificity of interval training. Specificity is important in all training forms.

The following table provides an outline of how the energy systems benefit in percentage increase from the varying training methods:

Energy system development between training methods

Training Method	Per Cent Development		
	Anaerobic Alactate	Anaerobic Lactate	Aerobic
Interval	10–30	30–50	20–60
Repetition	10	±50	±40
Long-distance	2	8	90
Fartlek	20	40	40
Sprint	90	6	4
Interval sprinting	20	10	70

The Warm-up

The three purposes of a warm-up are: to stretch the muscles, tendons and ligaments; to heat the body, especially the muscles and joints; and to stimulate the mind and body for the workout or competition to come.

The warm-up procedure is divided into three steps:

1. Dress in racing clothes. Carry out a last-minute check of all your equipment to make sure it's all working properly. Take on several short, fast and simple activities to keep mental sharpness up. For example, you could practise gear changes while warming up on your bike.

2. Ride easily and increase the pace slightly to the level where the body is warm and sweating lightly. However, always use a small gear in the process and concentrate on pedalling skills. Never put the body under excessive stress.

3. Practise some tactical manoeuvering which will be required for the coming event. This will heighten mental sharpness as much as physical preparation.

Acquiring Skills

The recipe for acquiring skills is correct training and conscientious practice. This is how champions appear to make their winning performances look simple, relaxed and precise.

There are two basic skills you should aim to develop — closed and open:

- **Closed skills** are those you use in a predictable and regula environment. They are habits which have become virtually instinctive, such as the motion of pedalling. Outside influences have little impact on their enactment.

- **Open skills** are called upon when an environment changes and there is no guarantee of predictability. Adaptability is vital here. One example of an open skill is the lead-out tactic in a bunch sprint. Climbing and descending are also open skills because of the changes in terrain.

Indoor Alternatives

■ The Gym

As with developing the energy systems, there are several key principles to strength training. They are:

- **Frequency**: Workouts need to be consistent and regular. About two to three times a week is ideal.

- **Overload**: In this context overload refers to the increase of resistance in a workout. It should be progressive with weight and repetitions increase — depending on the aim of your workout.

  If strength is the goal, then a recipe of low repetitions and a high load/weight is needed.

  If power endurance is needed, then high repetitions (up to 20) and a low load/weight is desired.

- **Specificity**: This refers to the development of muscles according to the manner in which they will be used.

■ Weight Training

Many people misunderstand the benefit of weight training. Some fear it will impede movement and therefore minimise power output. There is a lack of scientific reasoning to this — if anything, it can increase speed.

Cyclists with little muscular strength are often hit with relatively early fatigue in the various limbs and joints. It can even come before the oxygen system is strained. Lacking strength can also impede a rider's ability to acquire skills.

The act of cycling does build strength, but it cannot develop a rider's total potential level of strength. The body needs to be regarded as a total unit. This means that all parts need to be given strength — both the muscles needed for cycling and those supporting the muscles used.

The nervous system plays an integral part in developing muscle use. However, even then, if the muscle is weak it will not meet the demand given by the nervous impulse.

The neuromuscular system — the recruitment of muscle fibres for movement through the nervous system — varies in efficiency from person to person.

Similarly, in untrained muscles the diameter of fibres varies. In strength-building programmes smaller fibres develop to the size of the bigger ones (hypertrophy). So when strength and muscle mass is increased, the number of muscle fibres stays the same — but their increase in diameter makes the muscle size larger.

Research has also indicated that change in the central nervous system can stimulate muscle strength and endurance — even though this is not common.

Ten Tips to Weight Training

1 Include a 10 to 15 minute warm-up.

2 The first set of exercises should be of a high number (e.g. 10 to 15) using smaller weights (50%). Increase the weights and lessen the repetitions as you do more sets if building bulk and strength is the goal.

3 Increase weights and repetitions if muscle endurance is needed.

4 Use your own body weight if equipment is limited or not available — do push-ups and sit-ups.

5 In exercising, try to use the same motions as you use in cycling.

6 Vary the focus of hard work on different areas of the body. Alternate exercises between upper body, lower body, the trunk, etc.

7 Always record specific details of any workout and follow a programme under the strict guidance of a qualified trainer. This helps future assessment and evaluation of progress and averts injury.

8 Use isometrics regularly.

9 Develop strength before power in the legs.

10 Remember that a cyclist's upper body needs to be strong to enhance supportive muscle strength, but not large or bulky, so don't neglect your upper-body development.

■ Circuit Training

The purpose of circuit training is to develop strength, speed, agility, power, muscular endurance, flexibility and cardiovascular endurance.

Circuit training is based on a recipe of variety — involving intensity, duration and repetition. It should involve a series of specific cardiorespiratory and weight-resistance exercises in a set period of time.

It is a great off-season source of conditioning which offers many benefits:

- it is relatively short in duration, but high in stress;
- it is based on progressive development according to ability and condition;
- it is a form of conditioning in which the individual can easily gauge his/her development;
- it is conducted indoors so is not dependent on good weather.

Examples of Circuit Training

Circuit A is designed for athletes who rely on muscular strength. Hence it focuses on weight resistance. Circuit B focuses on cardiorespiratory demand.

Circuit A	Circuit B
1. Bench press	1. Running 400 metres (437 yards)
2. Bent-knee sit-ups	2. Push-ups
3. Knee extension	3. Bent-knee sit-ups
4. Lateral pull-down	4. Vertical jumps
5. Back hyperextension	5. Overhead press
6. Overhead press	6. Cycling (3 minutes)
7. Dead lift	7. Hip stretch
8. Arm curl	8. Skipping (1 minute)
9. Leg curl	9. Bent-over rowing
10. Upright rowing	10. Hamstring stretch
	11. Upright rowing
	12. Running 600 metres (656 yards)

Tips to Circuit Training

1 Sessions should be made up of between 6 to 15 stations. It should take you up to 30 minutes to complete each circuit.

2 Exercises focusing on one part of the body should be spread throughout the circuit to avoid overusing that particular muscle group.

3 Pay attention to doing the exercise properly. The full benefit of an exercise will only be attained through a quality effort. Being lackadaisical about it can even lead to injury.

4 Despite the above 'rule', participants should still aim to complete a circuit as fast as possible. There should not be any extensive break or rest period between each station change. Movement from one station to another should be the only moment of respite you get.

5 The number of repetitions of each exercise depends on your own ability — everyone has different physical limits.

■ The Indoor Trainer

This is a popular training tool for cyclists when the weather is either too poor to ride, or when they are injured (e.g. with a broken collarbone) and confined to limited conditioning programmes.

Nevertheless, while it may not be your first choice as a training tool, it is still a very effective one. The most common complaint about riding an indoor trainer is that it becomes boring! But you can develop your own escape from this — by using a personal stereo, watching television or just letting your imagination wander free.

The suggested exercises can be done on 'rollers' too, although they don't have the valuable resistance that indoor/wind trainers offer. Another advantage of indoor trainers is that they are more stable as the bike is attached to the machine either by the rear axle or front forks, whereas with rollers the bike sits on top. Whatever you use, your local bike shop dealer will be able to advise you on the models available.

The real benefit of an indoor trainer comes when you follow an individually tailored training programme. Its stability and the fact that it is indoors makes assessment of overload, the monitoring of heart rates and attention to style much easier.

Opposite are some examples of suggested workouts. Be aware, however, that these are training sessions which an advanced élite rider would tackle. They should be regarded only as a guide. If you are a beginner, start by doing 50% of the exercises and build up as your strength and ability develop. Be realistic about your ability. It is recommended that these sessions are done a *maximum* of three times a week.

Photocopy and laminate the programmes for easy reference while riding.

LEFT: foldable, magnetic-resistance indoor cycle trainer;
RIGHT: non-resistance cycle training rollers

Programme 1
Anaerobic Alactic Energy System

- Pedal revolutions per minute: 150 for sprinters / 130 for team pursuiters
- Time period for each effort: 15 seconds
- Relief time between efforts: 45 seconds, or heart rate of 120 to 140 beats per minute (bpm)
- Number of efforts per set: 10
- Relief time between sets: 5 minutes (drink water for hydration)
- Number of sets per session: 5
- Total number of efforts: 50
- Heart rate per effort: maximum effort (heart rate not applicable)

the **dean woods** MANUAL OF CYCLING

Programme 2
Anaerobic Alactic Energy System

To start, heart-rate maximum should be at about 170 to 175 bpm and increase each week to prescribed maximum. See the target heart rate graph under Interval Training on page 119 for a gauge as well. (You can also decrease the number of efforts if you wish.)

- Pedal revolutions per minute: 150 for sprinters / 130 for team pursuiters
- Time period for each effort: 20 seconds
- Relief time between efforts: 40 seconds, or heart rate of 120 to 140 bpm
- Number of efforts per set: 8
- Relief time between sets: 5 minutes, or when pulse drops below 120 bpm
- Number of sets per session: 5
- Total number of efforts: 40
- Heart rate per effort;   maximum effort (heart rate not applicable)

the **dean woods** MANUAL OF CYCLING

Programme **3**

Anaerobic Lactic Acid Energy System

To start, heart-rate maximum should be about 170 to 175 bpm and increase each week to prescribed maximum. (You can also decrease the number of efforts if you wish.)

- Pedal revolutions per minute: 100 to 130
- Time period for each effort: 1 to 2 minutes
- Relief time between efforts: 1 minute, or heart rate of 120 to 140 bpm
- Number of efforts per set: 5
- Relief time between sets: 5 minutes, or when pulse drops below 120 bpm
- Number of sets per session: 3
- Total number of efforts: 15
- Heart rate per effort: 85 to 95% of maximum heart rate

the dean
woods
MANUAL
OF CYCLING

Programme **4**

Anaerobic Lactic Acid Energy System

To start, heart-rate maximum should be about 170 bpm and increase each week to the prescribed maximum. (You can also decrease the number of efforts if you wish.)

- Pedal revolutions per minute: 120
- Time period for each effort: 2 to 2½ minutes
- Relief time between efforts: 2 minutes, or 120 to 130 bpm
- Number of efforts per set: 5
- Relief time between sets: 5 minutes
- Number of sets per session: 2
- Total number of efforts: 10
- Heart rate per effort: 85 to 90% of maximum heart rate

the dean
woods
MANUAL
OF CYCLING

Programme **5**
Aerobic Energy System

To start, heart-rate maximum should be about 170 bpm
and increase each week to the prescribed maximum.

- Pedal revolutions per minute: 120
- Time period for each effort: 5 to 6 minutes
- Relief time between efforts: 5 minutes, or 120 to 130 bpm
- Total number of efforts: 4
- Heart rate per effort: 80 to 90% of maximum heart rate

the
**dean
woods**
MANUAL
OF CYCLING

Programme **6**
Aerobic Energy System

After 2 to 3 weeks, it should be possible to increase work output at the same heart rates.
A great endurance conditioner, this programme can be done every day
— depending on your mental commitment!

- Pedal revolutions per minute: 90 for road cyclists / 100 for track cyclists
- Time period: up to 60 minutes
- Heart rate: 80 to 90% of maximum heart rate

the
**dean
woods**
MANUAL
OF CYCLING

Fatigue and Psychological Effects of Training

The *Oxford Dictionary* defines *fatigue* as weariness after exertion. It can be created by several factors:

- a build-up of lactic acid due to intense physical effort;
- depletion of blood-glucose levels after long-distance efforts;
- dehydration and electrolyte loss, which creates high body temperature;
- boredom from exercising long distances;
- general physical punishment from a rigorous training regime.

The loss of oxygen is a major element in this process, for without it the demand for energy cannot be met. And the less oxygen there is, the more glucose is only partially broken down to lactic acid.

BELOW: **Italy's Maurizio Fondriest, the 1993 World Cup winner, is a master in following the ideal recipe of rest and hard work in training.**
RIGHT: **No rider could better typify the skill of peaking than five-times Tour de France winner, Bernard Hinault of France.**

The build-up of lactic acid influences the cell environment to the extent that enzyme activity will break down, inevitably creating fatigue.

In low-intensity, long-distance training where glucose is slowly broken down in the muscles and liver, mental fatigue arises as the glucose needed for the brain is supplied from the liver. So when liver glucose stores diminish, so too does brain awareness.

In high-intensity, longer distance workouts and in a race the same effects are produced, although the process of fatigue is even quicker. This is the reason that coaches tell athletes to start a race at a manageable rhythm.

Basic Principles in Minimising the Onset of Fatigue

- Plan a ride or race according to the condition attained.
- Make sure carbohydrate and fluid stocks are full and replenished before and during a race as needed.
- Follow a training regime which balances the elements of overloading, specificity and rest/recovery. Starting a race already fatigued will lead to trouble.

Fatigue is a factor every rider will confront. It helps to know that the many physiological changes in your body which result from a training programme will help you to accommodate that stress.

There are increases in:

- ventilation efficiency;
- blood volume;
- oxygen-carrying capacity of the blood;
- heart size and stroke volume;
- carbohydrate and fat oxidation;
- muscular oxygen extraction;
- muscular capillary density;
- muscular enzyme activity in aerobic systems;
- lactic acid production at peak effort.

And there are decreases in:

- resting and sub-maximal heart rates and lactic acid production during sub-maximal exercise.

For any professional cyclist, the peak of the year is the Tour de France in July. Here, Spain's four-times winner, Miguel Indurain, leads Italy's Claudio Chiappucci and the field up the Col du Galibier in the Alps in the 1992 Tour.

Miguel Induraín cemented his status
as one of the greatest riders by adding
the World Hour record to his laurels
after winning the 1994 Tour de France.

Peaking

Peaking is the final touch to a training programme, and it can determine the cyclist's success or failure.

In many ways, it is the most delicate of facets in training to control. After weeks or months of intensity work, the body is now required to gradually ease the strain by tackling less work, replenishing energy supplies — and yet, at the same time, maintaining condition.

Tapering off will only be effective if a thorough training regime has been followed beforehand. The shorter the programme followed, the shorter the tapering-off period should be.

However, training should not stop totally before race day. It is important to keep your 'engine' ticking over. In races like the Tour de France, riders often begrudge rest days as they break up the race rhythm their bodies have adapted to in the two weeks prior to the event. It is not uncommon for competitors to train for up to four hours on these occasions instead!

Sprinters can peak two or three times in a training cycle. They usually require a longer tapering-off period of two to three weeks. Their event is an explosive power event, so these final weeks should see them undergo light road work, mixed with a short burst of track work.

Endurance riders can peak twice in a training cycle. They need to keep following their intensity levels in training up until one to three days before a race. Tapering off too early can diminish their competitive edge and lead to sluggishness and loss of condition.

An endurance rider's tapering-off period could follow this programme: for the last 9 to 12 days before a big race, implement a three-day macro-cycle. Split the cycle into one hard day, followed by one moderate and then one easy day. The easy day should be the day before competition.

OPPOSITE: Every team has its goals in the Tour de France. For the US-registered Motorola team, it has long been the team time trial. Here, in the 1991 race, Australia's Phil Anderson does his turn at the front, followed by Englishman Sean Yates and American Ron Kiefel.

7 The Race

The **Big Day**

The equipment is bought, the goals have been set
and you've done your training. The big day has
arrived. However, it is possible that your final
performance will be affected by your hour-to-hour
routine in the 24 hours *before* the race begins.
And similarly, your next performance can hinge
on the 24 hours *after* a race.

Pre and post-race routines not only make
sure that every element of your preparation and
eventual performance is covered, they also help
you to focus mentally on the race and cope with
its aftermath — be it positive or disappointing.

**Allan Peiper, Phil Anderson and Scott Sunderland
(left to right) start another stage in the 1993 Tour
of Ireland in positive mood, thanks to their efficient
pre-race routines.**

Pre-race

- Make sure all equipment, food and clothes needed for the race are either bought or repaired 48 hours beforehand. The day before should be spent resting — including a light training 'spin' — not chasing around shops for last-minute purchases.
- Give yourself plenty of time to pack and organise the next day's race equipment. Use a prepared check-list of everything you'll need to make sure nothing is forgotten.
- Review race and course details. Try to remember the crucial landmarks and difficulties of the race. Check the forecasted weather conditions.
- Drink plenty of fluids for the 24 hours before the race, although not so much that you become bloated. Try to stay away from alcohol too.
- The most important pre-race meal is dinner the night before. Eat a lot of carbo-hydrates, but not too soon before you go to bed.
- On race morning, don't eat too big a breakfast. Try to eat three hours before racing.
- If the race is in the afternoon, consume a hearty breakfast with an even balance of carbohydrates and protein.
- If the race is in the afternoon, go for a short, light spin in the morning to loosen up the leg muscles. If you're racing a time trial and are close to the route, ride over parts or all of the course slowly, paying particular attention to road surfaces — watch out for pot holes, or oil or loose gravel on corners and bends.
- Keep an eye on weather conditions. The forecast may have changed from the day before. On a time-trial route, watch out especially for changing wind patterns at various turns or rises of the course.
- Allow good time to travel to the race. At the minimum, arrive at least 1 hour before the start.
- Upon arrival, don't let yourself be distracted by others. You are there to race and, whatever the intentions of others, make sure you keep to your schedule. Time can slip away before a race more quickly than you can imagine!
- Locate available changing rooms, toilets and the race headquarters immediately.
- Change into race gear if you have not already done so. Make sure you keep casual or non-racing gear apart and in a separate, named bag. This will help efficient location of dry and clean gear to change into after the race.
- Organise racing equipment — especially the bicycle — and double-check it is all in working order.
- Give yourself or receive massage and required embrocations.
- Have a final drink and sign in as soon as you can, to give yourself several precious minutes of calm before the race starts.

Tactics

■ Who Does What

A road race can be like a game of chess on wheels. Each rider in a team has their own responsibility, tasks and level in the pecking order.

Each team has one or two leaders. Their selection either depends on general star status or — in teams without a top-salaried champion — the condition and form of those in the team on the day. Once those leaders have been selected, they become the pivotal force of every team member's attention that day. They are, in cycling jargon, 'protected riders'.

Some leaders may be riders who are good all-rounders and who have trained especially for the stage races and one-day classics. Others might be climbers who will either focus on racing for 'King of the Mountain' categories in tours or winning prestigious mountain stages and one-day races; or they could be sprinters who revel in the flat, speeding, massed-bunch sprints of stages and one-day classics.

Some riders, called 'domestiques', are employed on professional teams to literally service the needs of protected stars. Their 'services' can range from dropping back to a team car to collect or return clothes, food and drink, chasing down attacks or riding in front of their leader to protect them from cross and head-winds. They may even surrender their own wheel or bicycle should their leader suffer a puncture or mechanical trouble!

In between the top and bottom-ranked riders, there are several second-rung leaders who are also protected during the day up until the final, crucial moments of a race. Their allegiance will always be to the top leader, but should *that* rider suddenly be eliminated through unexpected fatigue, mechanical trouble or other circumstances, then the team will still have an alternative to pin its winning hopes on. If the number-one rider is racing strongly, then these second-rung leaders will still be fresh and primed to work for him or her when the real action hots up in the closing stages.

In among them all will be a team captain, or 'captain on the road'. The captain is usually an experienced veteran who does have occasional opportunities to win, yet whose main role is to coordinate the team's tactics. The captain is also the link between the riders and the team coach who usually follows behind the race in a convoy of team cars carrying spare wheels, bicycles, food and equipment. Captains are often older riders because of their greater experience from earlier racing days. They tend to be far more mature and rational under pressure and can maintain discipline amongst younger peers.

But the captain can't tell riders everything they need to know — there is still an onus on racers to understand the tactics of a bicycle race.

Sitting-on

Sitting-on, or 'riding a wheel', is something cyclists should learn as early as possible. It can be scary because it means that you ride very close to the cyclist in front of you who, in turn, can be riding within centimetres of the next cyclist. And on top of paying attention to what the rider in front is doing, it is also imperative that you keep an eye on the road, which could be blocked with parked cars or even a sudden crash.

In team time-trialling, sitting-on is a necessary discipline; in road racing, the benefits of sitting-on are tremendous. A rider following the wheel of another rider will travel at the same speed, but will use far less energy.

The best thing to do in a bunch is not to follow directly behind the rider ahead, but to ride slightly to their side, still very close. Whatever side is best will depend on wind direction. If the wind is from the right, then the left side of the front rider's rear wheel is better and vice versa.

Whichever side you choose, you will find a helpful wind-break or slipstream there. This will also help you to avoid riding into the back wheel of the rider in front, should they suddenly brake or slow down. In a big bunch where there may be numerous accelerations in a race, there is always much unexpected braking and sudden changes of line by other riders. It takes only the slightest break in concentration to discover — first-hand — the dangers of sitting-on.

The Australian team typifies the art of sitting-on during their sixth placed ride in the 1993 World Team Time Trial Championships at Oslo, Norway.

▇ Echelons

An echelon is the term given to a group of cyclists who are riding abreast. Their formation is normally caused by cross-winds. In these instances riders are positioned at approximately half a length behind and to the other side of the rider in front of them.

In Europe, echelon racing is very common. In countries like Australia where numbers are smaller, it's rare to see one. Racing in an echelon is experiencing cycling at its most demanding.

In head and tail-winds few echelon attacks will ever work. But once a bunch hits a cross-wind the race changes totally because there is only a small percentage of riders who will fit in a side-by-side formation across the road and manage to keep out of the wind.

There will be a split if the tail-end riders of the echelon can't keep up. They will drop back and often form a new echelon of their own. Many races in Europe see waves of up to four or five echelons form, with the trailing groups chasing desperately to join the one in front.

In these groups, there is no way one rider will ride at the front for the entire time — unless ordered to. It is generally accepted that every rider wanting to rejoin the leaders and stay away from those chasing will do their 'turn' at the front, where the wind will hit the echelon the hardest. After doing a turn a rider will ease up, veer out from the line and drop back to the rear of the group where there will be greater slipstream, or 'tow'.

There are two dangers in being at the back: firstly, a rider will be positioned badly to react to any attack in the front; secondly, they could inadvertently find themselves cast adrift should the middle of the bunch be split in half by a crash or the easing up of effort by one or two riders in the middle.

143

The field split into echelons during the 1986 Ghent–Wevelgem classic in Belgium.

Attacking

There are many good occasions to attack.

On a climb, if your legs are relatively fresh, the best place to attack is just before going over the top of a hill. The quicker a rider can get their momentum and rhythm going on the descent, the more time will be gained.

If you can't see over the crest of the hill it can be a touch frightening. But attacks call for daring!

In a time trial a maximum effort — akin to an attack — over the last kilometre could make all the difference, especially in a sport where winning margins can be so close between the top riders.

Another prime moment to attack may be just as an earlier break is about to be caught. Many in the chasing bunch will be tired and preparing for a rest after their efforts. By suddenly jumping away — perhaps even bridging the final metres of the pursuit — a rider may just grab that vital lead needed to forge ahead.

Breaks can also be successfully pulled off on twisting and narrow lanes, or on corners, where attacking riders can easily slip out of sight. On corkscrew roads, a single rider or small group will negotiate the turns at greater speeds than a larger chase group.

Attacks can also result from opportunity — an unexpected circumstance in the race may suddenly place the rider in an ideal position to get away. An example of this could be a crash. Crashes often split a bunch in two if the spill is in the middle. The riders in the front part of the group who escape the crash can then use this moment to attack.

In some circles, such an attack is not thought to be sporting. But this unwritten rule has often been ignored. Other moments are also regarded as off-limits to attackers. These might be during the feed zone when riders are slowing up deliberately to take a 'musette' — which contains extra carbohydrates in food and liquid form. Another taboo time to attack might be when a rival is delayed by a puncture or another mechanical problem. It can even be considered wrong to take advantage of a natural break en masse (i.e. which is agreed upon by the key members of the pack) early in the race. Still . . . cycling history recounts occasions when these codes have been broken too!

When an attack is made, it very rarely comes from a rider accelerating off the front — or from the front position of a pack. There's a simple reason for this — it gives too great an advantage to the rider behind, who will be in a position to follow any acceleration.

It's a better tactic to attack from behind as this will provide a chance of gaining the momentum of a break before anyone realises what is happening. This way too, there is a greater chance of jumping away without someone following.

One grave error many riders make when attacking is to only keep up the effort for 100 metres (109 yards) or so, and then to look around to see if anyone is chasing. If

Italian Claudio Chiappucci (left), just leading Colombian Oliviero Rincon in the 1992 Tour of Spain (right), is a rider who seeks any opportunity for a daring attack.

Frenchman Bernard Hinault leads the winning break in the 1984 Tour of Lombardy. His tactical wizardry and panache later brought him victory in this great one-day Italian classic over Belgian Ludo Peeters (hidden, and just behind Hinault) and Dutchman Tuen van Vliet (second from right).

there is, many of them sit up and drop back to the bunch. Not only is this a sign of lacking commitment, but it is also a waste of energy.

In Europe the tactic is for riders not to look around for a kilometre or so, especially if the break is into a side-wind, where they know the acceleration is putting the chasers under pressure. Even if they are caught, they'll know that they've played a part in tiring out their rivals — perhaps even weakening their resolve to pursue another break from their team soon afterwards.

It's also a good idea to use as much of the road space as possible during an attack. This will, of course, depend on enforced limits, with different countries having varying levels of clearance from traffic, etc. Look ahead and try to pick the smoothest and shortest line possible — especially in time trials.

Attacks don't necessarily only involve one person. Groups can make a break too. Sometimes there'll be riders in a group who will work and others who refuse to work or aren't able to because of fatigue. For the riders willing to work, there is always the risk that the others will sit-on, saving their energy and waiting for the finale to dig in and ride hard — just as the 'workers' are starting to fade.

Don't be fooled into towing others to the line. If everyone wants to work — including you — it's well worth the effort to do as many turns at the front as the others. But when there is a rider not wanting to contribute (for example, a sprinter wanting to wait until the last minute to attack) — it can be better to sit-up and let the break be caught before attacking again. This time the 'wheel sucker' might not get there!

Once a breakaway group has formed and it seems likely to stay to the finish, riders then face the task of matching their strength against their companions. Much of this depends on the course. On flat races a sprinter in any break stands a strong chance of winning if the group remains intact. A non-sprinter caught in a break with sprinters, however, would be better off trying to attack again, hoping to make it to the finish alone.

If there's an uphill finish, a rider who might not be a great climber but who packs an aggressive punch in a sprint might try to keep the group together until the final climb. Climbers, of course, would revel in mountainous courses where they could attack on every climb until they have shed the non-climbers.

When you're in a breakaway group, be wary of others bluffing. Some may say they're exhausted and try to fool their rivals by pretending they'd be happy just to make it to the finish in the group. Others may look as if they are finished as well. Some, on the other hand, manage to conceal their fatigue with stone-like expressions. Miguel Induraín is a master at this.

A great way to test any fellow breakaway companion before the finish is to launch one or two accelerations and then ease up. Observe their reactions — see who is the most responsive and who appears to suffer the most. Whatever you do, don't underestimate anyone!

Need Help?

There comes a moment in every cycle racer's life where a mechanical disaster strikes at a crucial moment — this could happen in a break, a chase, or as a peloton is in full flight at 60 kph (37 mph). When it does, there is a standard procedure to follow which can make the difference between winning and losing.

The first thing to remember when having any difficulty is not to tell anyone else but your team-mates or the personnel in the team car.

Most road races are followed by an entourage of team and mechanical support cars, ready to attend to the mechanical (and personal) needs of their riders. Problems can range from punctures, broken spokes or trouble with gears to a question of tactics.

When riders need assistance, they raise their arm for the race commissaire, or judge, who is following, to see. The commissaire then informs the personnel in the rider's team car that they are required for assistance. If possible, the commissaire will also tell the rider's 'support' what the need is — it could be something as trivial as wanting to return rain capes, or as potentially serious as a need for medical help. If it is the latter, a doctor would be informed as well.

Once the commissaire's message is received, the required team personnel will drive up to the commissaire's side of the road, from where they will be given the go-ahead to move alongside their rider in the bunch.

When the team car arrives, a rider should be in position at the side of the road. In countries where cars are driven on the right-hand side of the road, veer to that side, and vice versa. If the rider is still with the pack, they should also be at the rear. This alleviates congestion on the road and minimises the risk of someone being hit by a car or other riders.

Needy riders must be alert and ready to receive assistance. It is important to stay with the group after calling for help until your team car arrives. If the problem is a rear-tyre puncture, then it is OK to continue riding; if it's the front tyre, it's more difficult to continue — especially on a descent. If this happens, try to stay as close to the convoy of cars as is safely possible. It is illegal to take a tow from the slipstream of a car but, as long you don't spend too long behind any one car, race commissaires often let it slip.

In a race, the quickest remedy for a punctured tyre is a wheel change. Stop and wait for the team car to arrive. If it's a front-tyre puncture, save the mechanic time by taking out the wheel immediately. If it's a rear flat, before stopping, change down to bottom gear to assist wheel removal and replacement. Then, if the mechanic has not yet arrived, take the wheel out. Do this by standing alongside the bike, holding it upright by the saddle to make sure the front chain-ring doesn't slip off later.

After the mechanic has put the new wheel in and you've remounted for the chase, he or she will give you a push until you regain full acceleration again.

If a rider becomes detached from both the main group and the convoy, one or two team-mates will often drop back and help him or her to rejoin the race. In this instance, the riders will basically team-time-trial their way back to the peloton. This is a common situation in the last kilometres of a race where the peloton's speed is at its fastest and probably too fast for a lone rider to successfully chase.

A mechanic from the Spanish Artiach team repairs the rear derailleur for one of his riders during the 1993 Tour of Spain.

Post-race

If you can, have a helper or 'second' with you. Post-race situations are the moments of the racing day which can be the most confusing. By having someone with you, you'll be able to keep focused on doing what you have to do.

- Replenish lost fluids with a drink. Don't drink too quickly or too much. Avoid drinking alcohol immediately after a race.

- Wash yourself down with cologne or take a shower immediately if they are available.

- Change immediately into dry clothes and a pair of slippers or running shoes. Standing about in wet and dirty race gear can provoke a chill and you run the risk of picking up a cold.

- If you have won or are called to the podium, you will probably have to go there before you have a shower. If this is the case, remember to wear your official team or sponsor's colours and even products (e.g. sunglasses). This is the moment they expect you to be professional and provide publicity in return for their support.

- Check to see if you are required for any drug tests. If you have finished in the top three, you probably will have to undergo one. If not, you may be in the random checking list. If you are needed, don't forget the time limit which is normally 60 minutes after the race. Remember to take your race licence and any doctor's certificates for medication which contains allowable substances.

  You will be presented with an official form to sign as recognition that you have been summonsed; before being tested you have to sign another form before being given two sample bottles (for your urine sample) and another container in which you must urinate. In all controls, an official must actually witness the rider urinating in the container to ensure he/she doesn't cheat.

  If you have trouble urinating because of dehydration, you can drink more fluids to bring on the urge or, if it's a case of nerves, you can ask for permission to go for a short walk — although a drug control official must always be in your presence.

  Once you have urinated, you will then have to sign another form confirming that the procedure was carried out properly. If you have any doubts about the process, now is the time to say something. (*See Appendix on page 207 for the UCI's list of banned and restricted drugs.*)

- Make sure all racing gear and equipment has been packed and loaded into your car.

- Eat a light snack in the car if you face a long drive. Or have something at your hotel or house if dinner is scheduled for a couple of hours after you return.

- If possible, have a massage. Besides assisting recovery, this is also an opportune moment to have a post-mortem on the day's race. Another good way to help you think objectively about what went right or wrong is to keep a detailed training/racing log.
- Eat dinner, remembering to restore the nutrients and fluids you've lost.
- If celebratory or commiseratory consumption of alcohol is called for, take it in moderation. Remember . . . there is always the next race to think of!

As a new professional, Texan Lance Armstrong had a busy post-race schedule after winning the stage to Verdun in the 1993 Tour de France.

8 The Great Races

Cycling has come a long way since 31 May 1869 — the day an Englishman named James Moore won the first ever massed-start cycle race, Paris–Rouen.

More than a century on, all over the world — from Australia, the United States, Great Britain, France, Japan, South Africa, Taiwan, to even India and the Middle East — it's a safe bet that on nearly every day of the year somebody, somewhere, is putting their feet in the pedals and gearing up to race.

Whether it's for the Tour de France, a one-day classic, track pursuit, sprint or even a D-grade Sunday club race, the taste of competition lives within so many people.

While we can't list every race, it is possible to paint a picture of the *great* races in cycling. In many ways, this picture will illustrate a power pyramid of cycling which has Europe, unsurprisingly, firmly on top.

The peloton winds its way up one of the early ascents of the Tour of Lombardy classic in Italy.

The **Old World**

Cycle racing began in Europe. So it's only natural that the sport's traditional 'bloodline' comes from Europe where the biggest, most publicised and commercial races are held. Unlike other parts of the world, cycling *is* a major sport there.

European interest focuses mainly on the professional road-racing scene, which itself is divided between the tours and one-day races, of which a number of select events are labelled 'classics'. The track circuit comes to the fore in winter, which is in between the finish and start of road seasons.

The Tours

The term *tour* is given to a race which passes through various regions over a number of days. Tours are otherwise known as stage races, where the overall winner is the rider with the fastest accumulated time for the distance.

A tour is by no means a vacation! On the contrary, it is a punishing marathon which can last anything from a weekend to three weeks. Not only is it a test of a rider's all-round capacity to sprint, climb and time-trial, it is also a test of almost super-human endurance and — as modern racing becomes faster — recuperation.

■ Tour de France

The grandest and toughest stage race of them all. It is held every July, encompasses three weeks (although until 1987 it lasted for four weeks) and, of all the tours, draws the most publicity world-wide.

For all riders in the Tour, being one of the 200 competitors who line up at the start is a privilege. Just to compete in, let alone to finish, the Tour sets them above those who don't make the grade. Actually winning a stage or a category like the 'King of the Mountains' puts them in another league altogether. And the person who wins the prized 'maillot jaune', the leader's yellow jersey, is accorded an almost god-like status! To make the pressures of notoriety worthwhile there is also the virtual guarantee of a US$2 million-plus annual income to be made. On top of this the winner gets a prize purse of 2 million French francs (approximately A$600 000) which is given to team-mates and personnel to share.

Since the first Tour in 1903, French riders have won 35 of the 80 editions. The country next in line is Belgium with 18 wins, and Spain — thanks to Miguel Induraín's quadruple spree in 1991, 1992, 1993 and 1994 — with six. Australia's best result has been two fifth places in 1982 and 1985 achieved by Victorian Phil Anderson, who also won stages in 1982 and 1991 and spent 11 days in the yellow jersey.

To Europeans, and especially to the French, the Tour is as much a part of tradition as the French Revolution. It has only *not* been held during the two World Wars. Barely an afternoon passes every July without people in cafés, business offices and homes everywhere crowding round the television to watch the live coverage of 'Le Tour'.

It is not surprising that the Tour is so commercially driven today. It always has been, and its organisers, the Societé du Tour de France, don't hide the fact. It began in 1903 as a publicity stunt by Henri Desgrange for the French sports paper *L'Auto*. It is because the paper's pages were then yellow that the leader's/winner's jersey is yellow today.

Since that first six-stage 2428-kilometre (1509-mile) edition of the Tour there have been many changes, nevertheless. Its format hasn't always been the same. Today the Tour is usually about 21 stages long, because the race entourage stops and re-starts every day — unlike the early days when competitors would ride on into the night.

Another major change has been the make-up of the field. Up until the mid 1960s both individuals and national teams competed. And the very first Tour in 1903 began with only 60 riders, of whom 21 finished. Today the field is made up of 22 trade-sponsored teams with a maximum total number of 198 riders. While the number of finishers varies, the average is about 120.

The Tour's route changes each year. It is now a major end-of-season event when Tour organisers gather the European cycling media together every October to reveal next year's course. The purpose of the route change is to constantly create new challenges for riders, as well as to extract more money from the various regions visited. Towns and cities have to fight a bargaining battle to earn the 'honour' of having the Tour pass through their streets. It is particularly expensive for a town to host a stage start or finish. And for those towns wanting to stage the Tour start — usually a three-day affair — it can cost up to A$2.5 million!

The Tour de France may be the sport's 'holy grail', but there are two other major three-week tours which, although not as internationally influential, are just as significant in their home countries. They are the Tours of Spain and Italy — the Vuelta a España and Giro d'Italia respectively.

Vuelta a España

The Tour of Spain is the youngest of the 'big three'. It was first held in 1935 over 14 stages on a 3411-kilometre (2119-mile) course. To Spaniards — competitors and spectators alike — it is a national festival which challenges the Tour de France for razzmatazz.

The Vuelta isn't so popular among foreigners, though, and there are several reasons for this. Firstly, it began and continued during a period when the rest of Europe was engaged in a world war. Then, in the days of the Franco government, its staging was interpreted by some as a shop window for fascist propaganda.

It is also problematic in purely sporting terms: its traditional calendar slot has made the Vuelta an extremely demanding race for non-Spaniards who have just completed the spell of spring one-day classics in Belgium and France. Not only are most foreigners already fatigued, but the often cold and wet weather of northern Europe hardly prepares them for conditions in Spain, which can be extreme, raging heat suddenly snapping into a bitingly cold, snowy front. Foreigners also have to contend against Spanish riders and teams who are at their seasonal peak.

From its 48 editions up until 1994, Spaniards have won the Vuelta 21 times. Eight titles have gone to French riders, seven to Belgians, four to Italians, three to Swiss, two to Dutch and one each to German, Irish and Colombian riders.

There have been many tales of foreign riders falling victim to organised combines from local teams who prefer to help one of their own countrymen win — even if they are from another team! Five-times Tour de France winner Bernard Hinault of France won the Vuelta in 1978 and 1983 and came away claiming it was one of his hardest victories. And two-times runner-up Robert Millar of Scotland even saw a virtually assured win 'stolen' from him in 1985 when almost the entire Spanish contingent combined on the penultimate day to ride against him. He was race leader when the day began, yet by that afternoon, a break led by Spaniard Pedro Delgado had got more than six minutes up the road before Millar — surrounded and boxed in by silent Spaniards — received news of the attack from officials.

There have been two important phases to the Vuelta's recent development. The first was when the current race organisers, Unipublic, took over the race in 1982 after being co-organisers for three years from 1979. Unipublic's influence was as commercially driven as that of the Societé du Tour de France but, even with the oxygen of sponsorship, it was not until 1990 that international interest in the Vuelta began to grow.

The second phase was scheduled to take place in 1995. This was the controversial move to change the date of the Vuelta from May to September. Debate (sometimes ugly) over the change continues to this day, but in 1993 the UCI and Unipublic put their stamp of approval on the plan, believing the move would help the event's standing. While fans of year-round events will be robbed of an early three-week 'major tour', it was believed the move would create more interest from foreign competitors and the media.

However, the Vuelta still suffers because many big teams focus on the Tours of Italy or France. Up until 1994, Unipublic hadn't yet succeeded in getting Miguel

OPPOSITE: The 1990 Tour of Spain leaves the town of Segovia for the finish at Madrid on the final day.

Induraín to make his first return to the Vuelta battlefront since 1991 when he lost to another Spaniard — Melchior Mauri.

Furthermore, by staging the race in September, cycling administrators are hoping the Vuelta may become a 'grudge' race of sorts — a platform for those who have 'failed' in France or Italy to avenge their performances. This is unlikely, because it would be hard for riders to tackle such a long race competitively *after* a gruelling ordeal like the Tour de France. But it is feared that as the Vuelta is now held so soon after the world championships, it may run the risk of becoming obsolete. Time will tell.

Giro d'Italia

The Tour of Italy, or Giro, is probably the one major tour which has not undergone any dramatic change — nor has it needed to. Its slot in June is perfect for local teams wanting to tackle a spring classic programme and then peak for *their* national tour, or for those riders wanting to prepare for the Tour de France.

The Giro was first run in 1909, founded by the Italian sports daily, *Gazzetta dello Sport*, who are still organisers today. While it has never lacked a Latin bias, it has been a race traditionally fairer to foreign riders in recent years.

In the last ten years, up until and including 1994, Italians have won on only three occasions, with the last being Franco Chioccioli in 1991. Showing signs of the sport's increasing internationalism, six 'stranieri' (foreign) champions have won on seven occasions and have come from such diverse countries as Ireland (Stephen Roche / 1987), the United States (Andy Hampsten / 1988), France (Bernard Hinault / 1985 and Laurent Fignon / 1989), Spain (Miguel Induraín / 1992 and 1993) and Russia (Eugeni Berzin / 1994).

The Giro's timing is definitely an attraction for foreign riders. They come to the race expecting a strong national front, yet they can at least challenge it knowing they are prepared. This is often not the case with the Vuelta. Other advantages include better hygiene, dietary standards and weather than is generally the case in Spain.

Sponsors also reap greater returns from the Giro than they do at the Vuelta, simply because it is rated as the second biggest of the three major tours. This is the result of investment by Italian cycling manufacturers who sponsor teams from around the world. (This isn't the case in Spain.)

Competitors in the 1992 Tour of Italy ride through the spectacular scenery of the Dolomites — the mountain range of northern Italy where so often the race is won or lost.

The Giro has been held 77 times since its birth. And Italians have won on 54 occasions, the first foreign winner being Switzerland's Hugo Koblet in 1950. Other countries which have won the Giro are Belgium (seven victories), France (six), Switzerland (three), Luxemburg and Spain (two), and the US, Ireland and Russia (one).

There are other tours, ranging in length and prestige. Nearly every country in Europe has its own national tour, while many have regional tours as well, in which many valued titles are up for grabs. It is generally acknowledged that the fourth largest tour is the ten-day Tour of Switzerland in June.

After that comes an array of races ranging from six to eight days in length. There are season-opening events like the Ruta del Sol in Spain and the Tour Méditerranéen and Etoile de Bessèges in France; there are 'major' races like Paris–Nice in France and Tirreno–Adriatico in Italy, which act as headlining build-ups to the first classics, and there is a constant run of minor races, most of which precede a greater event on the calendar like the tours of France, Italy and Spain or the world championships.

The One-day Classics

As with the tours, the calendar of one-day races has its 'crème de la crème'. They are simply called the 'classics'. Many of them fall into a season-long World Cup competition of one-day events which is split into two terms — spring and autumn.

The 'monuments' of these races are: Milan–San Remo, the Tour of Flanders, Paris–Roubaix, Liège–Bastogne–Liège and the Tour of Lombardy. They may just be names to anyone not brought up on cycling, but in European households they have an almost religious significance because of their long heritage.

■ Milan–San Remo

First raced in 1907, Milan–San Remo in Italy in March is the first classic of the year and hence is called the 'Primavera'. It is a marathon at nearly 300 kilometres (186 miles), yet its notoriety comes not from its length but for the crescendo of excitement created from the decisive moves on the hills in the last 60 kilometres (37 miles) where the race follows the winding Mediterranean coastline to San Remo.

■ Tour of Flanders

This race in Belgium usually takes place two weeks after Milan–San Remo in early April. Yet it heralds the first of a bout of one-day races in northern Europe called the 'spring classics'. It first appeared on the calendar in 1913 and has since developed the honour of being known as one of the toughest of all classics. Not only is it long, at 265 kilometres (165 miles), but its terrain also demands a true 'all-rounder' for a winner. Riders have to do combat against wind, normally foul weather and an array of narrow, twisting country lanes and steep hills.

■ Paris–Roubaix

Created in 1896, this is the most prestigious race in its class, one of its two monikers being the 'Queen of the Classics'. The darker side of this punishing event is equally well described in its other label: the 'Hell of the North'. The name is due to the event's back-breaking stretch of cobblestones which make up about 55 kilometres (34 miles) of the route. Often contested in wet conditions, the sectors of loaf-sized Roman cobbles provoke a number of dramatic crashes and punctures. Riders either love Paris–Roubaix or hate it — and the relationship is born on a rider's first encounter.

■ Liège–Bastogne–Liège

Because it is the oldest of the major classics, this race is fittingly called the 'doyenne'. When it was born in 1892, however, it was an amateur race only. The creation of a

ABOVE: Steve Bauer (right) leads Sean Kelly (centre) and Eric Vanderaerden over the famous Koppenberg Climb of the 1986 Tour of Flanders. After 1987, organisers scrapped the climb, claiming it was too hard. BELOW: In the Arenberg Forest, pools of mud and water and slippery cobblestones await the field of the Paris–Roubaix.

THE GREAT RACES

professional edition came two years later. Its distinct trademark is the accordion of forested hills of the Belgian Ardennes near the German and Dutch frontiers. Traditionally it's been seen as a climbers' race, but recent editions have seen all-rounders win.

Tour of Lombardy

The fifth monument is at the tail-end of the season, and closes the World Cup. It is held in Italy in October. Also known as the 'Race of the Falling Leaves', since it is held during autumn, this monument of racing is a tough event. Part of the route is over hills and one or two smaller mountains around picturesque Lake Como. Another factor in the equation is its place at the end of the season — in late October most riders are on their last legs after ten months of classics and tours.

Complementing these five classics in the World Cup are five more one-day events: the Amstel Gold in Holland, the Championship of Zurich in Switzerland, the Leeds International in England, the Classico San Sebastián in Spain and Paris–Tours in France. Interspersing these, but without World Cup status, are such one-day races as Het Volk, Ghent–Wevelgem, Flèche–Wallonne and Paris–Brussels in Belgium, the Grand Prix of Frankfurt in Germany; and the Giro del Lazio, Milan–Turin and Tour of Piemonte in Italy.

There is only one one-day race which arguably surpasses any other — yet doesn't have a 'classic' tag to it. This is the World Professional Road Race Championship. Held every year at a different location, at the very end of a two-week spell of track and road world titles, the Professional crown is a veritable lottery. (After 1995, track and road world titles will be held at separate locations at different times.) While riders officially represent their country and race in national colours, many still abide by trade-team loyalties — unless they are in a winning position themselves!

The Track Circuit

Track racing in Europe is mainly a winter affair. The world championships may be in August (towards the end of the European summer), but for many trackmen and women, those titles mark the *start* of a season which doesn't really reach its peak until October.

The main racing events are the Six-day and Sprinters' Grand Prix circuits. The Open des Nations format, where eight-person national teams compete against each other over a variety of events, is also picking up in popularity.

Match sprinting has its own Grand Prix circuit. Two of the world's top sprinters are West Australia's Darren Hill (left) and Italy's Claudio Golinelli.

In the increasingly popular Open des Nations track racing format the team pursuit is a highlight event. The precision and speed of the Germans, here en route to winning the 4000-metre Team Pursuit in the 1992 Barcelona Olympics, shows why.

Six-day Racing

Six-day racing's origins go back to the turn of the century and to the United States, where cycling rivalled baseball in the popularity stakes. Today its feet are firmly fixed in Europe, with Germany being its power-base. The six-day calendar used to have as many as 17 races, but now it is generally down to 12 events. In a Six-day Race, riders pair up in two-person teams and over six nights of racing between 8 p.m. and 2–3 a.m. they compete in a variety of madisons, derny events and sprints, with one rider usually resting while the other races (except in the madison, where both riders compete).

Sprinters' Grand Prix

This is a recent addition to winter track racing. It is now a part of the six-day programme, although riders competing in the Grand Prix do not race in the six-day event as well. While providing the world's best sprinters with an income source from competition, the excitement of pushing, shoving and tactical one-upmanship in Grand Prix sprint racing is a real crowd-pleaser.

Six-day track racing's origin is in the US. Today, however, its home is in Europe in the winter season.

165

Women's Racing

Women's competition has a relatively brief life span. On a world-championship level, it started in 1958 with a 59-kilometre (37-mile) road race and an individual pursuit and match sprint race on the track. And it was not until 1984 at Los Angeles that it became a fixture in the Olympic programme.

Women's racing has a full calendar of events lasting from March until November. The focal points of this calendar are in Europe, the main road events being:

- Three Days of Vendée: held in early April, it is a three-stage race.
- Tour de l'Aude in France: held in early to mid May, it is a ten-day stage race officially ranked in the 'Super' category by the UCI.
- Omloop't Molenheike in Holland: held in mid to late May, this is also a Super category stage race, although it's held over four days.
- Tour of West Norway: a five-day Super category race held in late June, or early July.
- Tour of Italy Féminin: a national-classed stage race held over seven days in early July.
- Tour Cycliste Féminin in France: not to be mistaken with the now-defunct Tour de France Féminin, this race is still the biggest stage race on the women's calendar. Lasting two weeks, it is a Super category race.

Men's Amateur and Open Racing

The following are the leading amateur and open (amateur *and* professional) stage events on the calendar. For amateurs — and new professionals eligible to race in open events — these races are not only major events in their own right, but also important stepping stones to future careers.

- Tour of Normandy, France (amateur — March / 8 days)
- Settimana Ciclista Bergamasca, Italy (open — April / 11 days)
- Circuit Franco-Belge, Belgium (amateur — April / 6 days)
- Giro Regioni Primavera d'Italia (amateur — April / 6 days)
- Peace Race, Czechoslovakia (amateur — May / 10 days)
- Tour of Sweden (open — June / 7 days)
- Tour of Austria (amateur — June / 10 days)
- Tour of Germany (amateur — July / 11 days)
- Regio Tour, Germany (open — August / 7 days)
- Tour de l'Avenir, France (open — September / 11 days)

The New World

Europe is not the only place for top-level racing. The sport is rapidly expanding to new frontiers.

Australia

Australia has become an increasingly popular venue internationally. End-of-year professional events like the Vic Health Herald–Sun Tour of Victoria have seen more and more Europeans competing. And in New South Wales, the Pacific Power Commonwealth Bank Classic in October has cemented its reputation as one of the biggest amateur stage races on the international calendar. As from 1995, it will be Open as well.

Other major domestic events in Australia include Melbourne–Warnambool, Grafton–Inverell, Goulburn–Liverpool and the Tasmanian Christmas Carnival track series. Adelaide is also the location for some great track racing where packed crowds fill the recently built Superdrome at meetings between October and March.

The Pacific Power Commonwealth Bank Classic is now one of Australia's leading international races.

167

North America

North America has long been targeted for serious expansion. While attempts to stage a World Cup race at Montreal in Canada fizzled out after several years (due to financial restraints), stage races in the United States have been reasonably successful. Admittedly the Coors Classic has disappeared after initially receiving the 'thumbs up' from visiting Europeans in 1986, but it looks as though the Tour Du Pont is heading towards greener pastures. Until recently it clashed with the Tour of Spain but, with the Spanish event's shift to September in 1995, organisers are hoping the Tour Du Pont will now become *the* major May stage race on the calendar.

Great Britain

Cycling in the British Isles has had its share of mixed fortunes. In England the Kellogg's Tour has survived, thanks to its calendar position as a warm-up for the Leeds International World Cup race, which takes place two days afterwards. And nothing could have been better to promote the sport than the three-day passage of the Tour de France in 1994.

Yet one of the saddest blows to British cycling came in the same year when the Milk Race — one of the toughest pro-am stage races in the world — was called off due to the loss of sponsorship from the British Milk Marketing Board. The Milk Race tradition lives on in Scotland and Ireland, though, where Milk Boards there continue to sponsor stage races. Another big pro-am race in Britain is the Tour of Lancashire.

Ireland

As with the Coors Classic in the US, the Nissan Classic of Ireland was just becoming a favourite among visiting European teams when its financial support collapsed and the event was shelved after 1992. Moves are afoot to bring the race back.

Japan

Japan is a country in which cycling interest is centred on the professional league of Keirin racing, where spectators bet on riders, as they would on horses or greyhounds.

Major races in other countries which mirror the global expansion of cycling include the Ruta del Mexico, the Tour of Taiwan, the Rapport Tour of South Africa, the Tour of Israel and the Tour of Burkino Fasso in Africa.

What the Jerseys Mean

- **yellow jersey** (maillot jaune) — overall leader in the Tour de France (and many other stage races)
- **pink jersey** (maglia rosa) — overall leader in the Tour of Italy
- **golden jersey** (maillot amarillo) — overall leader in the Vuelta a España
- **rainbow jersey** (maillot arc en ciel) — world champion

Points Competition

This is based on accumulated stage finish placings and — sometimes — placings at intermediate sprints. Points are awarded for each placing with the rider with the most points being the eventual winner. It is often a sprinter who wins.

- **green jersey** — leader of points competition in the Tour de France
- **purple jersey** — leader of points competition in the Tour of Italy
- **blue jersey** — leader of points competition in the Tour of Spain

Climbers' Competition

Points are awarded according to riders' placings at the summit of every mountain.

- **red and white polka-dot jersey** — leader of climbers' competition, or King of the Mountains in the Tour de France
- **green jersey** — winner of climbers' competition in Tours of Italy and Spain

Inter-Giro

This is a competition included in the Tour of Italy; the winner wears a blue jersey. It is judged on every rider's position and their time at an intermediate mark in each day's stage. It is a general classification, but decided at approximately the half-way mark of the stages. This is the second highest paying category in the Tour of Italy.

9 The Great Racers

Every sport has its champions. And in many ways the build-up of interest in cycle racing is due to the feats of those champions who match up to and conquer the demands of top-level international competition.

The reality is that only a small percentage of the cycling fraternity will ever make it into the upper echelons of the sport. This, however, is a factor which only enhances the magnitude of the victories by those who do make the 'cut'.

History has provided us with hundreds of great winners — and losers. However, it is by the achievements of those who have *won* that all standards are set. Whether we make it to the top or not, those standards give everyone something to look up to.

Who are those pioneers of cycling? Where do they come from? And who has done what? The following pages introduce you to some of the most prominent riders in the disciplines of road **R**, track **T** and cyclo-cross **C** racing.

From Europe, the United States and Australia, these are just a few of the champions you'll find people talking about today.

Miguel Induraín revealing unforeseen attacking flare in the stage to Hautecam in the Pyrenees during the 1994 Tour de France. The only rider who could follow was Frenchman Luc Leblanc, who benefited from the 'tow' to win the stage.

Don Allan R T

24 September 1949–

Present Status: Retired

Nationality: Australian

Career Highlights

First in Tour of Spain stage in 1975

First in European Madison Criterium in 1980

First in 17 Six-day Races

Finished Tour de France in 1974 (103rd) and 1975 (85th)

Phil Anderson R

20 March 1958–

Present Status: Retired

Nationality: Australian

Career Highlights

First Australian to claim Tour de France yellow jersey (one day) in 1981 and win in Young Riders category; stape win in 1982 (and ten days in yellow jersey) and 1992.

First in Tour of Italy stage in 1989 and 1990, including Inter-Giro blue jersey

First in Commonwealth Games Road Race in 1978

First in Commonwealth Games Team Time Trial in 1994

First in Tour de l'Aude in 1981 and 1983

First in Kellogg's Tour of Britain in 1991 and 1993

First in Tour Méditerranéen in 1985 and 1991

First in Tour of Romandy in 1989

First in Tour of Switzerland in 1985, including one stage win

First in Blois–Chaville in 1986

First in Dauphiné Libéré in 1985

First in Milan–Turin in 1987

First in Amstel Gold Race in 1983

First in Championship of Zurich in 1984

First in Grand Prix of Frankfurt in 1984 and 1985

First in Grand Prix d'Isbergues in 1992

First in Nissan Classic of Ireland in 1992

First in Sicilian Week in 1991

Second in Liège–Bastogne–Liège in 1984

Second in Paris–Tours in 1990

Third in Liège–Bastogne–Liège in 1983 and 1989

Fifth in Tour de France in 1982 and 1985

Ninth in Tour de France in 1983

Jacques Anquetil R

1 January 1934–18 November 1987

Nationality: French

Nickname: Maître Jacques

Career Highlights

First in Tour de France in 1957, 1961, 1962, 1963 and 1964, including 16 stage wins from eight Tours

First in Tour of Italy in 1960 and 1964, including six stage wins

First in Tour of Spain in 1963, including one stage win

World Hour Record-breaker in 1956 (46.159 kilometres (28.681 miles) indoor)

First in Bordeaux–Paris in 1965

First in Dauphiné Libéré in 1963 and 1965

First in Ghent–Wevelgem in 1964

First in Liège–Bastogne–Liège in 1966

First in Paris–Nice in 1957, 1961, 1963, 1965 and 1966

First in Grand Prix des Nations in 1953, 1954, 1955, 1956, 1957, 1958, 1961, 1965 and 1966

Moreno Argentin R

17 December 1960–

Present Status: Retired

Nationality: Italian

Career Highlights

First in Tour de France stage in 1990 and 1991

First in Tour of Italy stage in 1993 (two wins), achieving sixth place overall

First in World Professional Road Championship in 1986

First in Tour of Denmark in 1985

First in Tour of Flanders in 1990

First in Tour of Lombardy in 1987

First in Flèche–Wallonne in 1990, 1991 and 1994

First in Liège–Bastogne–Liège in 1985, 1986, 1987 and 1991

First in Italian Professional Road Championship in 1986

172

Lance Armstrong R

18 September 1971–

Nationality: American

Career Highlights
First in Tour de France stage in 1993
First in World Professional Road Championship
   in 1993
First in Tour of Galicia stage in 1992
First in Tour of Sweden stage in 1993
First in Grand Prix of Marostica, Italy, in 1992
First in Settimana Bergamasca in 1991
First in Trophy Laigueglia in 1993
First in US Amateur Road Championship in 1991
First in US Professional Road Championship
   in 1993
First in US Thrift Drug Classic in 1992 and 1993
First in US $1m-Triple Crown series in 1993
First in US West Virginia Classic in 1993
Second in Classico San Sebastián in 1994
Second in Tour Du Pont in 1993
Second in Liège–Bastogne–Liège in 1994
Seventh in World Professional Road
   Championship in 1994

Steele Bishop T

29 April 1953–

Present Status: Retired
Nationality: Australian

Career Highlights
First in World Professional Pursuit Championship
   in 1983
Sixth in World Professional Pursuit Championship
   in 1982
Eighth in World Professional Pursuit
   Championship in 1991

Chris Boardman R T

6 August 1968–

Nationality: English

Career Highlights
First in Tour de France Prologue Time Trial in 1994,
   including three days in leader's yellow jersey
World Hour Record-breaker in 1993 (52.270
   kilometres (32.479 miles) / indoor)
First in World Pursuit Championship in 1994

First in World Time Trial Championship in 1994
First in Olympic Games Pursuit in 1992
First in Tour of Murcia Time Trial in 1994,
   including stage in leader's jersey
First in two stages of Dauphiné Libéré, including
   three days in leader's jersey
First in Chrono des Herbiers in 1993
First in Duo Normand Time Trial in 1993
First in Grand Prix of Eddy Merckx in 1993
Third in World Pursuit Championship (Open)
   in 1993
Sixth in World Amateur Pursuit Championship
   in 1991
Eighth in World Amateur Pursuit Championship
   in 1990

Gianni Bugno R

14 February 1964–

Nationality: Italian

Career Highlights
First in Tour of Italy in 1990
First in Tour de France stage in 1988 two
   in 1990, and one in 1991
First in World Cup in 1990
First in World Professional Road Championship
   in 1991 and 1992
First in World Rankings in 1990
First in Tour of Flanders in 1994
First in Milan–San Remo in 1990
First in Milan–Turin in 1992
First in Classico San Sebastián in 1991
First in Italian Professional Road Championship
   in 1991
First in Wincanton Classic in 1990
Second in Tour de France in 1991
Third in Tour de France in 1992

Beryl Burton R T

1937–

Present Status: Retired
Nationality: British

Career Highlights
World Record-breaker of 20 Kilometres in 1960
   (28:58.40 / (standing start) outdoor)
World Record-breaker of 3 Kilometres twice
   in 1964 (4:16.60 and 4:14.90 / outdoor)

173

First in World Pursuit Championship in 1959,
1960, 1962, 1963 and 1966
First in World Road Race Championship in 1960
and 1967
Second in World Road Race Championship in 1961

Maria Canins R

4 June 1949–

Present Status: Retired

Nationality: Italian

Career Highlights
First in Tour de France Féminin in 1985, including
first in climbers' competition, and 1986,
including six stage wins and first in climbers'
competition
Second in Tour de France Féminin in 1987,
including first in climbers' competition
Second in Women's World Road Race
Championship in 1982 and 1985
Third in Women's World Road Race
Championship in 1989

Connie Carpenter-Phinney R

26 February 1957–

Nationality: American

Career Highlights
First in Women's World Pursuit Championship
in 1983
First in Olympic Games Women's Road Race
Championship in 1984
Second in Women's World Pursuit Championship
in 1982
Second in Women's World Road Race
Championship in 1977
Third in Women's World Road Race
Championship in 1981

Claudio Chiappucci R

28 February 1963–

Nationality: Italian

Career Highlights
First in Tour de France stage in 1991, including
King of the Mountains title, 1992 (King of the
Mountains title again) and 1993
First in Tour of Italy stage in 1994

174

First in Tour of Basque Country in 1991
First in Milan–San Remo in 1991
First in Classico San Sebastián in 1993
Second in Tour de France in 1990, including
eight-day spell in leader's yellow jersey,
and 1992
Second in Tour of Italy in 1991 and 1992
Third in Tour de France in 1991
Third in Tour of Italy in 1993

Danny Clark T

30 August 1951–

Nationality: Australian

Nickname: Super Athlete

Career Highlights
First in World Professional Keirin Championship
in 1980 and 1981
First in World Professional Motor-paced
Championship in 1988 and 1991
First European Derny Championship in 1985, 1986
and 1989
First in European Omnium Championship in 1978,
1979, 1983 and 1987
First in European Madison Championship in 1980
and 1989
First in 68 Six-day Races (third highest overall)
Second in Olympic Games 1000-metre Time Trial
in 1972
Second in World Professional Keirin
Championship in 1982 and 1983
Second in World Professional Motor-paced
Championship in 1985
Second in World Professional Points
Championship in 1981
Third in World Professional Motor-paced
Championship in 1990
Third in World Professional Points Championship
in 1990

Fausto Coppi R

1919–1960

Nationality: Italian

Nickname: Il Campionissimo (Super
Champion)

Career Highlights
First in Tour de France in 1949 and 1952,
including nine stage wins from three Tours

First in Tour of Italy in 1940, 1947, 1949, 1952 and 1953

World Hour Record-breaker in 1942 (45.798 kilometres (28.457 miles) indoor)

First in World Professional Pursuit Championship in 1947 and 1949

First in World Professional Road Championship in 1953

First in Tour of Lombardy in 1946, 1947, 1948, 1949 and 1954

First in Flèche–Wallonne in 1950

First in Milan–San Remo in 1946, 1948 and 1949

First in Paris–Roubaix in 1950

First in Grand Prix des Nations in 1946 and 1947

First in Italian Professional Road Championship in 1942, 1947, 1949 and 1955

First in Tour of Lombardy in 1974 and 1976

First in Flèche–Wallonne in 1971

First in Liège–Bastogne–Liège in 1970

First in Milan–San Remo in 1973, 1978 and 1979

First in Paris–Brussels in 1981

First in Paris–Roubaix in 1972, 1974, 1975 and 1977

First in Tirreno–Adriatico in 1972, 1973, 1974, 1975, 1976 and 1977

First in Belgian Professional Road Championship in 1969 and 1981

First in Championship of Zurich in 1975

First in Het Volk in 1969 and 1979

Second in World Amateur Cyclo-cross Championship in 1969

Eric de Vlaeminck ▉R▉ ▉C▉

23 August 1945–

Present Status: Retired

Nationality: Belgian

Career Highlights

First in Tour de France stage in 1968

First in World Professional Cyclo-cross Championship in 1966, 1968, 1969, 1970, 1971, 1972 and 1973

First in Tour of Belgium in 1969

First in Paris–Luxemburg in 1970

First in Championship of Flanders in 1969

First in Circuit of the Flemish Ardennes in 1969

Third in World Professional Cyclo-cross Championship in 1977

Roger de Vlaeminck ▉R▉ ▉C▉

24 August 1947–

Present Status: Retired

Nationality: Belgian

Nickname: Le Gitan (Gypsy)

Career Highlights

First in Tour of Italy points classification in 1972 and 1975

First in World Amateur Cyclo-cross Championship in 1968

First in World Professional Cyclo-cross Championship in 1975

First in Tour of Flanders in 1977

Etienne de Wilde ▉R▉ ▉T▉

23 March 1958–

Nationality: Belgian

Career Highlights

First in Tour de France stage in 1989 and 1991

First in World Points Championship (Open) in 1993

First in Belgian Professional Road Championship in 1988

First in Etoile de Bessèges in 1989

First in European Omnium Championship in 1989

First in Grand Prix Wielerrevue in 1988 and 1991

First in Het Volk in 1989

First in 28 Six-day Races

Tony Doyle ▉T▉

19 May 1958–

Nationality: English

Career Highlights

First in World Professional Pursuit Championship in 1980 and 1986

First in European Madison Championship in 1985 and 1989

First in 23 Six-day Races

Second in World Professional Points Championship in 1987

Second in World Professional Pursuit Championship in 1984, 1985 and 1988

Andre Dufraisse ◙

30 June 1926–

Present Status: Retired

Nationality: French

Career Highlights

First in World Cyclo-cross Championship (Open) in 1954, 1955, 1956, 1957 and 1958

First in French Cyclo-cross Championship (Open) in 1955, 1956, 1958, 1959, 1961, 1962 and 1963

Second in World Cyclo-cross Championship (Open) in 1951 and 1952

Third in World Cyclo-cross Championship (Open) in 1951, 1952, 1953, 1961, 1962 and 1963

Laurent Fignon ◙

12 August 1960–

Present Status: Retired

Nationality: French

Nickname: The Professor

Career Highlights

First in Tour de France in 1983, including one stage win, and 1984, including five stage wins; one stage win in 1987, 1989 and 1992

First in Tour of Italy in 1989

First in World Rankings in 1989

First in Tour of the European Community in 1988

First in Tour of Holland in 1989

First in Flèche–Wallonne in 1986

First in Milan–San Remo in 1988 and 1989

First in Criterium International in 1982 and 1990

First in French Professional Road Championship in 1984

First in Grand Prix de Cannes in 1982

First in Grand Prix des Nations in 1989

Urs Freuler ◙◙

6 November 1956–

Nationality: Swiss

Career Highlights

First in Tour de France stage in 1981

World Amateur Record-holder for 1000 Metres in 1980 (1:5.582 / indoor)

World Record-holder for 500 Metres in 1981

(28.48 sec / indoor)

World Record-holder for 1000 Metres in 1981 (1:6.79 / outdoor and 1:6.603 / Indoor)

First in World Professional Keirin Championship in 1983 and 1985

First in World Professional Points Championship in 1981, 1982, 1983, 1984, 1985, 1986, 1987 and 1989

First in Tour of North-west Switzerland in 1985 and 1988

First in European Omnium Championship in 1981, 1982 and 1988

First in European Sprint Championship in 1982

First in 18 Six-day Races

Thomas Frischknecht ◙

17 February 1970–

Nationality: Swiss

Career Highlights

First in World Junior Cyclo-cross Championship in 1988

First in World Amateur Cyclo-cross Championship in 1991

Third in World Amateur Cyclo-cross Championship in 1990 and 1992

Alf Goullet ◙

5 April 1891–

Present Status: Retired

Nationality: Australian

Career Highlights

First in 15 Six-day Races

Winner of many national sprint titles before emigrating in 1913 to the United States (where he still lives), where he concentrated on the six-day scene

Andy Hampsten ◙

7 April 1962–

Nationality: American

Career Highlights

First in Tour of Italy in 1988

First in Tour de France in Best Young Riders category in 1986

First in Tour de France stage in 1992, including
Alpe d'Huez stage

First in Tour of Galicia in 1993, including
one stage win

First in Tour of Romandy in 1992, including
one stage win

First in Subida Urkiola One-day Race in Spain
in 1990

First in Tour of Switzerland in 1986 and 1987; one
stage win in 1990

Second in Tour of Switzerland in 1990 and 1991

Third in Tour of Switzerland in 1990

Fourth in Tour de France in 1986 and 1992

Fifth in Tour of Italy in 1992

Eighth in Tour de France in 1991 and 1993

Reg Harris T

1920–1992

Nationality: English

Career Highlights

World Record-holder for 1000 Metres
(Professional) in 1949 (1:9.8 / outdoor), 1952
(1:8.6 / outdoor and 1:9.0 / indoor), 1955
(1:8.9 / indoor) and 1957 (1:8.0 / indoor)

First in World Amateur Sprint Championship
in 1947

First in World Professional Sprint Championship
in 1949, 1950, 1951 and 1954

First in Grand Prix de Paris (Amateur) in 1946

First in Grand Prix de Paris (Professional) in 1951
and 1956

Second in World Professional Sprint
Championship in 1956

Third in World Professional Sprint Championship
in 1953

Paul Herijgers C

22 November 1962–

Nationality: Swiss

Career Highlights

First in World Cup in 1993

First in World Cyclo-cross Championship (Open)
in 1994

First in Belgian Cyclo-cross Championship in 1993

Bernard Hinault R

14 November 1954–

Present Status: Retired

Nationality: French

Nickname: Le Blaireau (Badger)

Career Highlights

First in Tour de France in 1978, 1979, 1981, 1982
and 1985, including 28 stage wins from eight
Tours

First in Tour of Italy in 1980, 1982 and 1985

First in Tour of Spain in 1978 and 1983

First in World Professional Road Championship
in 1980

First in Tour of Lombardy in 1979 and 1984

First in Tour of Luxemburg in 1982

First in Dauphiné Libéré in 1977, 1979 and 1981

First in Flèche–Wallonne in 1979 and 1983

First in Ghent–Wevelgem in 1977

First in Liège–Bastogne–Liège in 1977 and 1980

First in Paris–Roubaix in 1981

First in Amstel Gold Race in 1981

First in Coors Classic in 1986

First in Four Days of Dunkirk in 1984

First in French Professional Road Championship
in 1978

First in Grand Prix des Nations in 1977, 1978,
1979, 1982 and 1984

First in Super Prestige Season series in 1979,
1980, 1981 and 1982

Michael Hubner T

8 April 1959–

Nationality: German

Career Highlights

World Amateur Record-holder for 200 Metres
in 1986 (10.118 sec / outdoor)

World Record-holder for 500 Metres in 1991
(26.11 sec / indoor)

First in World Amateur Sprint Championship
in 1986

First in World Professional Sprint Championship
in 1990 and 1992

First in World Professional Keirin Championship
in 1990, 1991 and 1992

First in Grand Prix de Paris in 1989 and 1990

177

Miguel Induraín R

16 July 1964–

Nationality: Spanish

Nickname: Big Mig

Career Highlights

First in Tour de France in 1991, 1992, 1993 and 1994, including stage wins in 1989, 1990, 1991 (two), 1992 (three), 1993 (two) and 1994 (one)

First in Tour of Italy in 1992 and 1993, including two stage wins in 1993

World Hour Record-breaker in 1994 (53.040 kilometres (32.957 miles) / indoor)

First in Tour de l'Avenir in 1986

First in Tour of Catalonia in 1988

First in Tour of the Mining Valleys in 1986

First in Paris–Nice in 1989 and 1990

First in Classico San Sebastián in 1990

First in Spanish Professional Road Championship in 1992

Third in Tour of Italy in 1994

Gordon Johnson T

1 August 1946–

Present Status: Retired

Nationality: Australian

Career Highlights

First in World Professional Sprint Championship in 1970

Second in World Professional Sprint Championship in 1972

Sean Kelly R

2 May 1956–

Present Status: Retired

Nationality: Irish

Nickname: King Kelly

Career Highlights

First in Tour of Spain in 1988; points victory in 1979

First in Tour de France points classification in 1982, 1985 and 1989, including five stage winsfrom four Tours

First in World Cup in 1989

First in World Rankings concurrently in 1985, 1986, 1987 and 1988

First in Tour of Basque Country in 1984, 1986 and 1987

First in Tour of Catalonia in 1984 and 1986

First in Tour of Lombardy in 1983, 1985 and 1991

First in Tour of Switzerland in 1983 and 1990

First in Blois–Chaville in 1984

First in Ghent–Wevelgem in 1988

First in Liège–Bastogne–Liège in 1984 and 1989

First in Milan–San Remo in 1986 and 1992

First in Paris–Nice in 1982, 1983, 1984, 1985, 1986, 1987 and 1988

First in Paris–Roubaix in 1984 and 1986

First in Catalan Week in 1988

First in Criterium International in 1983, 1984 and 1987

First in Grand Prix des Nations in 1986

First in Nissan Classic of Ireland in 1985, 1986, 1987and 1991

First in Super Prestige Season series in 1984, 1985 and 1986

Michael Kluge C

25 September 1962–

Nationality: German

Career Highlights

First in World Amateur Cyclo-cross Championship in 1985 and 1987

First in World Professional Cyclo-cross Championship in 1992

Second in World Professional Cyclo-cross Championship in 1993

Greg LeMond R

26 June 1961–

Present Status: Retired

Nationality: American

Nickname: Le Ricain (slang for 'Americain')

Career Highlights

First in Tour de France in 1986, 1989 and 1990, including three stage wins in 1985, 1986 and 1989

First in World Professional Road Championship in 1983 and 1989

First in Tour de l'Avenir in 1982

First in Tour Du Pont in 1992

First in Dauphiné Libéré in 1983

First in Coors Classic in 1985
First in Super Prestige Season series in 1983
Second in Tour de France in 1985
Third in Tour de France in 1984

Roland Liboton C

6 March 1957–

Present Status: Retired

Nationality: Belgian

Career Highlights
First in World Amateur Cyclo-cross Championship
in 1978
First in World Professional Cyclo-cross
Championship in 1980, 1982, 1983 and 1984
First in Belgian Amateur Cyclo-cross
Championship in 1979
First in Belgian Professional Cyclo-cross
Championship in 1980, 1981, 1982 and 1984
Second in World Professional Cyclo-cross
Championship in 1981

Jeannie Longo R T

31 November 1958–

Nationality: French

Career Highlights
First in Tour de France Féminin in 1987, 1988
and 1989
Multi World Record-breaker at all distances from
3 Kilometres to 1 Hour
First in Women's World Points Championship
in 1989
First in Women's World Pursuit Championship
in 1986, 1988 and 1989
First in Women's World Road Championship
in 1985, 1986, 1987 and 1989
First in Coors Women's Classic in 1981, 1985,
1986, including three stage wins and climbers'
competition, and 1987
First in Women's Tour of Columbia in 1987
and 1988
First in Women's Tour of Texas in 1984 and 1985
Second in Tour de France Féminin in 1986,
including four stage wins
Second in Women's World Road Championship
in 1993
Third in Women's World Time Trial Championship
in 1994

Freddy Maertens R

13 February 1952–

Present Status: Retired

Nationality: Belgian

Career Highlights
First in Tour of Spain in 1977, including points
classification
First in Tour de France points classification
in 1976, 1978 and 1981, including eight stage
wins in 1976, two in 1978 and five in 1981
First in World Professional Road Championship
in 1976 and 1981
First in Blois–Chaville in 1975
First in Ghent–Wevelgem in 1975 and 1976
First in Paris–Brussels in 1975
First in Amstel Gold Race in 1976
First in Belgian Professional Road Championship
in 1976
First in Championship of Zurich in 1976
First in Grand Prix des Nations in 1976
First in Grand Prix of Frankfurt in 1976
First in Het Volk in 1977 and 1978
First in Super Prestige Season series in 1976
and 1977

Eddy Merckx R

17 June 1945–

Present Status: Retired

Nationality: Belgian

Nickname: The Cannibal

Career Highlights
Competed in 1800 races, winning 525
First in Tour de France in 1969, 1970, 1971, 1972
and 1974, including 35 stage wins
from seven Tours
First in Tour of Italy in 1968, 1970, 1972, 1973
and 1974, including 25 stage wins
First in Tour of Spain in 1973, including six stage
wins
World Hour Record-breaker in 1972 (49.431
kilometres (30.714 miles) indoor)
First in World Professional Road Championship
in 1967, 1971 and 1974
First in Tour of Flanders in 1969 and 1975
First in Tour of Lombardy in 1971 and 1972
First in Tour of Switzerland in 1974, including
five stage wins

179

THE GREAT RACERS

First in Dauphiné Libéré in 1971
First in Flèche–Wallonne in 1967, 1970 and 1972
First in Liège–Bastogne–Liège in 1969, 1971, 1972, 1973 and 1975
First in Milan–San Remo in 1966, 1967, 1969, 1971, 1972, 1975 and 1976
First in Paris–Roubaix in 1968, 1970 and 1973
First in Amstel Gold Race in 1973 and 1975
First in Belgian Professional Road Championship in 1970

Robert Millar R

13 September 1958–

Nationality: Scottish

Career Highlights
First in Tour de France stage in 1983, 1984, including King of the Mountains title, and 1989
First in Tour of Catalonia in 1985
First in Dauphiné Libéré in 1990
First in Kellogg's Tour of Britain in 1989
Second in Tour of Italy in 1987, including one stage win
Second in Tour of Spain in 1985 and 1986, including one stage win
Second in Tour of Romandyin 1990 and 1991
Second in Tour of Switzerlandin 1986 and 1990
Fourth in Tour de France in 1984

Russell Mockridge R T

18 July 1928–15 September 1958

Nationality: Australian

Career Highlights
First in Olympic Games Tandem Championship in 1952 (with Lionel Cox)
First in Olympic Games Kilometre Time Trial Championship in 1952
First in Tour du Vaucluse in 1955
First in Australian Road Race Championship in 1947
First in Grand Prix de Paris in 1952 and 1953
Finished Tour de France in 1955 (64th)
Mockridge was killed during the 1958 Tour of Gippsland in Victoria, Australia, when he crashed into a bus.

Daniel Morelon T

28 July 1944–

Present Status: Retired
Nationality: French

Career Highlights
World Amateur Record-holder for 500 Metres in 1976 (28.75 sec / indoor)
First in World Amateur Sprint Championship in 1966, 1967, 1969, 1970, 1971, 1973 and 1975
First in World Tandem Championship in 1966 (with Pierre Trentin)
First in Olympic Games Tandem Championship in 1968 (with Pierre Trentin)
First in Olympic Games Sprint Championship in 1968 and 1972
First in European Sprint Criterium in 1981
First in French Amateur Sprint Championship in 1964, 1966, 1967, 1968, 1969, 1970, 1971, 1972, 1973, 1974, 1975, 1976 and 1977
First in Grand Prix de Paris in 1965, 1967, 1968, 1970, 1971 and 1977
First in Noumea Six-day Races in 1977
Second in World Professional Keirin Championship in 1980
Second in Olympic Games Sprint Championship in 1976

Francesco Moser R

19 June 1951–

Present Status: Retired
Nationality: Italian
Nickname: Checco

Career Highlights
First in Tour of Italy in 1984
First in Tour de France stage in 1975
World Hour Record-holder in 1984 (50.808 kilometres (31.570 miles) outdoor and 51.151 kilometres (31.783 miles) outdoor)
First in World Professional Pursuit Championship in 1976
First in World Professional Road Championship in 1977
First in Tour of Lombardy in 1978
First in Flèche–Wallonne in 1977
First in Milan–San Remo in 1984
First in Paris–Roubaix in 1978, 1979 and 1980
First in Tirreno–Adriatico in 1980 and 1981
First in Italian Road Championship in 1975, 1979 and 1981

Koichi Nakano T

14 November 1955–

Present Status: Retired

Nationality: Japanese

Career Highlights
First in World Professional Sprint Championship in 1977, 1978, 1979, 1980, 1981, 1982, 1983, 1984, 1985 and 1986

Gary Neiwand T

4 September 1966–

Nationality: Australian

Career Highlights
First in World Keirin Championship (Open) in 1993
First in World Sprint Championship (Open) in 1993
First in Commonwealth Games Sprint Championship in 1986, 1990 and 1994
Second in Olympic Games Sprint Championship in 1992
Third in World Amateur Sprint Championship in 1991
Third in Olympic Games Sprint Championship in 1988
Fifth in World Sprint Championship in 1987

John Nicholson T

22 June 1949–

Present Status: Retired

Nationality: Australian

Career Highlights
First in World Professional Sprint Championship in 1975 and 1976
Second in World Professional Sprint Championship in 1974
Third in World Professional Sprint Championship in 1977

Graeme Obree T

11 September 1965–

Nationality: Scottish

Career Highlights
World Hour Record-breaker in 1993 (51.596 kilometres (32.060 miles) / indoor) and 1994 (52.713 kilometres (32.754 miles) / indoor)

First in World Pursuit Championship (Open) in 1993
Fourth in Florence–Pistoia Time Trial in 1993

Sir Hubert Opperman R T

29 May 1904–

Present Status: Retired

Nationality: Australian

Career Highlights
World Record for 1000 Kilometres in 1928
World Record for 1000-miles Motor-paced Race in 1932
World Unpaced 24-hour Record-holder in 1939
Record for Lands End–John o'Groat's (UK) in 1934
First in Paris–Brest–Paris in 1931
First in Boule d'Or in 1928
Twelfth in Tour de France in 1931
Eighteenth in Tour de France in 1928

Connie Pareskevin-Young T

4 July 1961–

Nationality: American

Career Highlights
First in Women's World Sprint Championship in 1982, 1983, 1984 and 1990
Second in Women's World Sprint Championship in 1985
Third in Women's World Sprint Championship in 1986, 1987 and 1991
Third in Olympic Games Women's Sprint Championship in 1988

Sid Patterson R T

10 August 1927–

Present Status: Retired

Nationality: Australian

Career Highlights
World Record-holder for 'flying' 1000 Metres in 1952 (Professional) (1:4.0 / outdoor)
First in World Amateur Pursuit Championship in 1950
First in World Professional Pursuit Championship in 1952 and 1953

First in World Amateur Sprint Championship
in 1949
First in 16 Six-day Races
Third in World Professional Sprint Championship in
1951

Rene Pijnen [T]

3 September 1946–

Present Status: Retired

Nationality: Dutch

Nickname: Marathon Man

Career Highlights
First in Tour of the North in 1969
First in European Derny Criterium in 1978
First in European Madison Championship in 1983
and 1986
First in European Madison Criterium in 1974,
1975, 1977, 1981 and 1982
First in Grand Prix de Cloture in 1969
First in Grand Prix de Fourmies in 1974
First in 72 Six-day Races (second highest overall)

Daniele Pontoni [C]

1968–

Nationality: Italian

Career Highlights
First in World Amateur Cyclo-cross Championship
in 1992
Third in World Amateur Cyclo-cross Championship
in 1991 and 1993

Hugh Porter [T]

27 January 1940–

Present Status: Retired

Nationality: English

Career Highlights
First in World Professional Pursuit Championship
in 1968, 1970, 1972 and 1973
Third in World Amateur Pursuit Championship
in 1963

Peter Post [R] [T]

20 November 1933–

Present Status: Retired

Nationality: Dutch

Nickname: The Showman

Career Highlights
World Record-holder for 5 Kilometres in 1962
(6:07.02 / indoor)
First in Paris–Roubaix in 1964
First in Dutch Professional Road Championship
in 1963
First in Dutch Pursuit Championship in 1957, 1958
and 1959 and 1961
First in European Derny Criterium in 1962, 1963,
1964, 1965, 1966, 1967, 1969 and 1970
First in European Madison Criterium in 1964, 1967
and 1969
First in European Omnium Criterium in 1964
First in European Pursuit Criterium in 1963
First in 65 Six-day Races (fourth highest overall)
Second in World Professional Pursuit
Championship in 1963
Third in World Professional Pursuit Championship
in 1962

Bruno Risi [T]

6 September 1968–

Nationality: Swiss

Career Highlights
First in World Amateur Points Championship in
1991
First in World Professional Points Championship in
1992
First in World Points Championship (Open) in 1994
First in 6 Six-day Races (two years as professional)
Second in World Amateur Points Championship in
1990

Roger Riviere [R] [T]

1936–1977

Nationality: French

Career Highlights
First in Tour de France stage in 1959 (two stages)
and 1960 (three) (before crashing on a
mountain descent which fractured his back
and ended his career)

World Hour Record-holder in 1957 (46.923 kilometres (29.156 miles) indoor and in 1958 (47.346 kilometres (29.419 miles) indoor)
First in World Professional Pursuit Championship in 1957, 1958 and 1959
First in French Amateur Pursuit Championship in 1956
Second in Grand Prix des Nations in 1959
Third in Dauphiné Libéré in 1959

Stephen Roche R

28 November 1959–

Present Status: Retired
Nationality: Irish

Career Highlights
First in Tour de France in 1987, and three stage wins from three Tours (1985, 1987 and 1992)
First in Tour of Italy in 1987
First in World Professional Road Championship in 1987
First in Tour of Basque Country in 1989
First in Tour of Corsica in 1981
First in Tour of Romandy in 1983 and 1984
First in Tour of Valencia in 1987
First in Paris–Nice in 1981
First in Criterium International in 1985 and 1991
First in Etoile des Espoirs in 1981
First in Four Days of Dunkirk in 1990

Tony Rominger R

27 March 1961–

Present Status: Scheduled retirement after 1996
Nationality: Swiss

Career Highlights
First in Tour of Spain in 1992, 1993 and 1994
World Hour Record-breaker twice in 1994 (55.291 kilometres and (34.356 miles) / indoor) (53.832 kilometres and (33.449 miles) / indoor)
First in Tour of Basque Country in 1992, 1993 and 1994
First in Tour of Lombardy in 1989 and 1992
First in Tour Méditerranéen n 1989
First in Tour of Romandy in 1991
First in Paris–Nice in 1991 and 1994
First in Tirreno–Adriatico in 1989 and 1990

First in Grand Prix of Eddy Merckx in 1994
Second in Tour de France in 1993

Patrick Sercu R T

27 June 1944–

Present Status: Retired
Nationality: Belgian
Nickname: The Phenomenon

Career Highlights
Three stage wins in Tour de France in 1974, including green points jersey, and one stage win in 1977
World Record-holder for 1000 Metres in 1964 (Amateur) (1:06.76 / indoor), 1972 (Professional) (1:02.46 / outdoor) and 1973 (1:02.46 / outdoor)
First in World Amateur Sprint Championship in 1963
First in World Professional Sprint Championship in 1967 and 1969
First in Olympic 1000-metre Time Trial in 1964
First in 88 Six-day Races (standing record)

Rob Spears T

1893–1950

Nationality: Australian

Career Highlights
First in World Professional Sprint Championship in 1920
First in Grand Prix de Paris in 1920, 1921 and 1922
First in two Six-day Races
Second in World Professional Sprint Championship in 1921 and 1922

Gary Sutton R T

27 March 1955–

Present Status: Retired
Nationality: Australian

Career Highlights
First in World Amateur Points Championship in 1980
Second in World Professional Points Championship in 1982, 1984 and 1989

Klaus-Peter Thaler **R** **T** **C**

14 May 1949–

Present Status: Retired
Nationality: German

Career Highlights
First in Tour de France stage in 1977 and 1978
First in World Amateur Cyclo-cross Championship
     in 1973 and 1976
First in World Professional Cyclo-cross
     Championship in 1985 and 1987
First in Tour de Levant in 1980
Second in World Amateur Cyclo-cross
     Championship in 1974 and 1975
Second in World Professional Cyclo-cross
     Championship in 1980
Third in World Professional Cyclo-cross
     Championship in 1978 and 1983

Rebecca Twigg **R** **T** **C**

26 March 1963–

Nationality: American

Career Highlights
First in Women's World Pursuit Championship
     in 1982, 1984, 1985, 1987 and 1993
Second in Women's World Road Race
     Championship in 1983
Second in Olympic Games Women's Road Race
     Championship in 1984
Third in Olympic Games Women's Pursuit
     Championship in 1992

Adri van der Poel **R** **T** **C**

17 May 1959–

Nationality: Dutch

Career Highlights
First in Tour de France stage in 1987 and 1980
First in Tour of Flanders in 1986
First in Blois–Chaville in 1987
First in Liège–Bastogne–Liège in 1988
First in Paris–Brussels in 1985
First in Amstel Gold Race in 1990
First in Championship of Zurich in 1982
First in Dutch Professional Cyclo-cross
     Championship in 1990 and 1992

First in Dutch Professional Road Championship
     in 1987
Second in World Professional Cyclo-cross
     Championship in 1985, 1988, 1989, 1990
     and 1991
Second in World Professional Road Championship
     in 1983
Third in World Professional Cyclo-cross
     Championship in 1992

Rik van Looy **R**

20 February 1932–

Present Status: Retired
Nationality: Belgian
Nickname: The Emperor

Career Highlights
First in World Professional Road Championship
     in 1960 and 1961
First in Tour of Flanders in 1959 and 1962
First in Tour of Lombardy in 1959
First in Flèche–Wallonne in 1968
First in Ghent–Wevelgem in 1956, 1957 and 1962
First in Liège–Bastogne–Liège in 1961
First in Milan–San Remo in 1958
First in Paris–Roubaix in 1961, 1962 and 1965
First in Paris–Tours in 1959 and 1967
First in Belgian Professional Road Championship
     in 1958 and 1963

Leontin van Moorsel **R** **T**

23 March 1970–

Nationality: Dutch

Career Highlights
First in Tour Cycliste Féminin in 1992 and 1993,
     including three stage wins
First in Women's World Pursuit Championship
     in 1990
First in Women's World Road Race Championship
     in 1991 and 1993
First in Women's Tour de l'Aude in 1991
First in Women's Tour of the European
     Community in 1992
Second in Women's Tour of the European
     Community in 1993, including three stage wins

184

Kathy Watt R T

11 September 1964–

Nationality: Australian

Career Highlights
First in Olympic Games Women's Road Race
   Championship in 1992
First in Commonwealth Games Women's Pursuit
   Championship in 1994
First in Commonwealth Games Women's Road
   Race Championship in 1990 and 1994
First in Australian Women's Individual Pursuit
   Championship in 1988, 1990, 1991, 1992, 1993
   and 1994
First in Australian Women's Road Race
   Championship in 1992, 1993 and 1994
First in Australian Women's Time Trial
   Championship in 1992, 1993 and 1994
First in Canberra Women's Milk Race in 1994,
   including five stage wins and climbers'
   competition
Second in Olympic Games Women's Pursuit
   Championship in 1992
Second in Commonwealth Games Women's
   Pursuit Championship in 1990
Third in Women's Tour of Italy in 1990

Dean Woods R T

22 June 1996–

Nationality: Australian

Career Highlights
World Champion in 3000-metre Individual Pursuit
   in 1983
World Champion in 3000-metre Individual Pursuit
   in 1984
First in Olympic Games 4000-metre Team Pursuit
   in 1984
First in Commonwealth Games 4000-metre
   Individual Pursuit in 1986
First in Commonwealth Games 4000-metre Team
   Pursuit in 1986
First in Commonwealth Games 4000-metre Team
   Pursuit in 1994
First in Grenoble Six-day Race in 1994
National Champion in 4000-metre Individual
   Pursuit in 1994
National Record-holder in 4000-metre Individual
   Pursuit in 1994 (27.67 sec / indoor)

Second in World Professional Pursuit
   Championship in 1989
Second in Commonwealth Games 10-mile Scratch
   Race in 1986
Second in 30-kilometre Point score Race in 1983
Third in Commonwealth Games 40-kilometre
   Points Race
Fourth in World 4000-metre Individual Pursuit
   in 1987
Fourth in Olympic Games 4000-metre Individual
   Pursuit in 1984

Albert Zweifel C

7 June 1949–

Present Status: Retired

Nationality: Swiss

Career Highlights
First in World Professional Cyclo-cross
   Championship in 1976, 1977, 1978, 1979
   and 1986
First in Swiss Cyclo-cross Championship in 1976,
   1977, 1979, 1980, 1981, 1982, 1983 and 1984
Second in World Professional Cyclo-cross
   Championship in 1975, 1982 and 1983
Third in World Professional Cyclo-cross
   Championship in 1981 and 1984

10 The Cyclist's Wardrobe

Having the correct clothing is vital. You need the right clothing to feel comfortable, as well as to protect you from the elements. And dressing sensibly will help to prevent heat loss and the risk of colds.

A cyclist almost needs two wardrobes — one for the winter and one for the summer. If you are cycling regularly in the heat of summer, make sure that your cycling wardrobe is well stocked with an assortment of clothes. For basic hygiene, cycling clothes should be washed every day, especially at this time of year, when residual sweat can lead to infection if you have an open cut or graze. Wearing dry clothing after racing is important too, to avoid catching cold.

Try to be conscious of the colour of your clothing too. Of all your garments the two which can protect you the most (apart from the helmet) are the jersey and cap. A white or light-coloured cycling jersey will absorb the heat much less than a dark-coloured one. The same goes for light-coloured cycling caps, which can have an added cooling effect when worn after being drenched in water and wrung out. It may be worth buying a light-coloured pair of shorts. However, if you're short of money, invest in a light-coloured jersey first.

Don't neglect the variety of climates and temperatures you may encounter. For example, Australia may be a 'sunburnt' country, but there are still wet and cold periods and — in certain places, such as north-east Victoria — snow and blizzards. So, wherever you plan to cycle, make sure you check the weather conditions and take along what clothing you need.

Don't be tricked into buying the cheapest clothing available. Everyone has limits on their spending, of course, but it's not worth having clothing made from poor-quality material. Cheaper garments sometimes have faults which can lead to tearing, thus exposing your body to the elements and possible injury. By spending a few extra dollars you can purchase clothing which really *does* protect you.

Many people buy imported products from Europe where cycling is a major sport and where clothes are made for the extreme and varying conditions there. While you'll pay more for these imported products, they can be thought of as an investment in terms of quality. Naturally, if locally made items are of equal quality and cost the same price — or less — then buy them.

For winter or pre-season training, kit up with thermal gear — a sleeveless suit or jacket, leg and arm-warmers, a rain jacket and a waterproof, wool-lined hat which can be worn under the helmet. Thermal clothing has many advantages. It keeps you warm while also allowing the skin to 'breathe' — that is, when you perspire, the sweat is absorbed by the material and kept from the skin so you don't get that sticky, wet feeling you have when you wear a cotton T-shirt, for example. Thermal gear is also light and hence there is limited (if any) restriction to movement which pure wool garments — however effective — can't offer.

However many layers of gear you put on is really up to you. To begin with, it's best to start with a thin vest made of wool and acrylic. (It's very hard to find pure wool these days.) Then wear acrylic cycling shorts ('knicks'), ideally with a bib-and-brace design where the material pulls up over your lower back: these will protect your joints from the cold when you are bending forward. With these basic items of thermal clothing you will have a good foundation of protection.

Then add what clothes you feel are necessary. In training, if the weather seems unpredictable, wear layers and garments which can easily be taken off. Layers also prevent chafing. You may want to wear a short-sleeved jersey and use arm-warmers which can be taken off if the weather improves, or you could wear long-sleeved tops (up to two or three in severe winters!) and leg-warmers if you choose not to wear long cycling tights. If it's certain to be cold, stick with long jerseys and thermal jackets.

When to wear thermal protective gear depends on your body's metabolism. A general rule of thumb is to wear thermal leg and arm-warmers until the temperature reaches about 20°C (68°F). Some cyclists, though, like to wear them for the first hour while warming up, even if it's over 20°C, to get the blood circulation going. (In Australia it rarely, if ever, becomes cold enough to wear leg-warmers during a race.)

Helmets

The most important piece of safety equipment you need. There are many brands on the market with varying prices, which can be confusing. Here are two key rules to follow: first, make sure the helmet you buy is officially recognised by industry manufacturing standards; second, don't try and cut costs by buying the cheapest helmet — the hospital fees as a result of a shoddy helmet not providing the safety you need will cost you a lot more!

It is, of course, recommended that you always wear a helmet. Helmet laws vary around the world. Their use is recommended in all countries, although some places are stricter than others. And Australia is arguably the strictest of them all. Australian law states that all cyclists must wear a hard-shell helmet whether they are racing, training, touring, or even if they are only going to the local corner shop. Failure to do so incurs on-the-spot fines.

Clockwise from top:
Netti Stream Hardcore
with foam liner;
Bell Avalanche (MTB);
and the Bell Image
Pro (road).

There are various types of hard-shell helmets for specific cycling forms. However, all models — which are generally made of polystyrene foam — should achieve an adequate combination of safety, lightness, aerodynamism and ventilation. Many events like pursuiting and the 'kilo' time trial require riders to wear aerodynamic helmets. However, the helmet you have for road cycling will suffice in other events like the sprint, points and motor-paced events.

Apart from Europe, most helmet laws do not accept leather 'hairnets'. In Europe they are only worn by professional cyclists who are still permitted to use them under the laws of the Union Cycliste Internationale.

The most cumbersome-looking helmets are those used in road cycling, although there has been much improvement in the appearance factor in recent years. The biggest complaint has been the problem of heat and ventilation when riding hills or mountains — a factor which really only confronts riders in events like the Tour de France when they are in the Alps or the Pyrenees.

In time trials and track endurance events like the pursuit or triathlons, the focus is on aerodynamism — hence the 'teardrop' style so frequently seen.

Mountain-biking helmets are more akin to road helmets, although many mountain-bike helmets also have a visor above the brow to block out the sun and to protect you from rain. Some of the most reliable brands of helmet are Giro, Specialised and Brancale.

Eye-protectors

Sunglasses with dark lenses will block out the sun and damaging ultra-violet rays. Clear-lensed glasses will enhance vision in wet, overcast and dark conditions. Both types of lenses will also provide protection from splinters of loose gravel, dust and insects. Some recommended brands are Oakley, Bollé and Cebe.

Jackets

In a cold wind, instead of wearing a plastic rain jacket over your clothes, it is best to wear a wind jacket. Rain jackets are only good in heavy rain. No matter how cold it is, because they are made of plastic, you will become too hot. Wind jackets allow for some ventilation and the chance for your body to 'breathe'.

A recommended brand which gives you the benefit of both rain and wind protection is Goretex. They also make a vest which fits over the head. These are great, because you don't have to wear too many layers of clothing underneath them which can add extra and unwanted weight to carry when wet. They also maintain dryness and warmth while allowing for maximum ventilation.

Undershirts

If it's really cold, a cyclist might wear one jersey and two — or even three — undershirts. Some people use T-shirts as undershirts, but this is not really ideal. T-shirts tend to stay wet from perspiration and can give you a chill. It is best to use clothing which absorbs the sweat, thus keeping your body dry.

CHECK LIST

Basic Equipment for Regular Training

- 1 pair cycling shoes
- 4 pairs socks
- 3 pairs knicks
- 3 short-sleeved cycling jerseys
- 1 long-sleeved cycling jersey
- 6 undershirts
- 1 hard-shell helmet
- 2 pairs racing mitts
- 1 pair thick cold-weather gloves
- 2 pairs leg-warmers
- 1 pair arm-warmers
- 1 pair sunglasses (with changeable dark/light lenses if possible)
- 1 wind jacket
- 1 rain jacket
- 1 Goretex jacket (if affordable)
- Goretex vest

Naturally you can expand this list. But with the above as your basic equipment, you're ready to go training in all conditions, safely and comfortably.

189

THE CYCLIST'S WARDROBE

There are synthetic-wool undershirts available which are quite good for this. If it is very hot and dry, then it is OK not to wear an undershirt; just wear your cycling jersey. If rain is expected, though, then you should wear an undershirt because dampness, added to the wind-chill factor, can make you cold.

Jerseys

The cycling jersey itself is often made from synthetic material too. In a race, you may be confined to wearing your club or team colours but, when training, wear brightly coloured jerseys. This is because when it gets dark bright colours will be more visible (white isn't necessarily ideal because it can get dirty more easily and even blends into the surrounding terrain).

How many cycling jerseys you should have is an open question. Many cyclists collect jerseys, while others ride with one or two favourites until they almost drop off. Ideally, it is best to have at least one short and one long-sleeved jersey. This not only gives you something to wear if one is being washed, it also gives you another layer to put on in chillier conditions.

190

Shorts

Lycra shorts are recommended for their flexibility and comfort. You can get shorts in thermal material too, but you don't really need them because leg-warmers almost come up to the top part of the thigh and while riding a cyclist is bent over the handlebars, protecting the thighs and crutch area from any wind chill. And the commonly used bib-and-brace design means that the bib portion acts as another layer of protection for the lower torso.

ABOVE: For warmer conditions short-sleeved jerseys and short-legged cycle knicks are both practical and comfortable. OPPOSITE: In cool conditions more protection is necessary and long-sleeved jerseys and long-legged knicks will retain more body heat.

The only problem with shorts is that in the wet, you can get your backside wet from the water flicking up from the rear wheel. This is a problem which can be alleviated by putting a mudguard on the back wheel.

For training and racing, you should have about three or four pairs of shorts. In training, shorts will wear out quickly — so keep two sets separate for racing only. This will maximise use of your clothes and also help to keep them clean, especially the chamois crutch section.

If you're not a heavy sweater, you can get two days' wear out of your cycling clothes before washing them, but never take risks with the chamois crutch. If possible, wash this area by hand or, if not, use a washing-machine at a low temperature setting. Try to let the shorts dry slowly in the fresh air or in front of a heater (when put in a tumble-dryer the crutch can become hardened or torn by the heat).

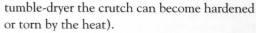

Thanks to a chamois crutch it is not necessary to wear anything underneath cycling shorts. However, the risk is that when dirt or grit get into the shorts, it can grind into the skin from the chamois. Saddle sores are a common result. Today the crutch area in a pair of shorts is often made from a synthetic material — or even terry-towelling. The main benefit of these materials is that they can be machine-washed and dried more easily. However, the very best shorts to have are still the ones with the traditional leather chamois crutch.

Many riders treat the leather crutch area of their shorts with creams. You don't need to do this if you're only cycling for one or two hours a day. But if you have a sensitive skin, if the surface you're cycling on is rough or if you're going at high speeds (which can create friction), you may benefit from using a cream.

Shoes

One of the most expensive items in a cyclist's wardrobe. They can cost up to A$300 for a good pair. It will depend on what level you're training or racing at. Remember, though, that badly fitted shoes can create injury to joints and muscles.

Everyone's feet are different — some people have flat feet, others have a very high arch. The only way to find out which shoes are best for your feet is to try out several pairs.

The two biggest differences between the cycling shoe and the running shoe is that cycling shoes have hard, stiff soles and cleats, or shoe-plates. A hard sole increases the effectiveness of the pedalling motion. Using running shoes is OK for recreational cycling on a mountain bike or even a road bike (if it's not on a regular basis), but for regular riders, proper cycling shoes are vital.

You'll also need to think about cleats (the piece of shoe which connects it to the pedal).They come in various designs, depending on the brand of shoe and the pedal. There are two types: the traditional cleat is used with pedals which have a leather toe-strap; the more modern 'strapless' version locks into the pedal by a ski-binding system. Positioning the cleat correctly in both types is extremely important. This will maximise pedal motion and avoid the risk of muscle injuries which can occur by wrongly positioned shoe-plates. Ask an experienced cyclist or the attendant at the cycling shop to help secure the correct position.

Another development in shoe design is the use of a velcro fastening strap instead of shoe laces. Some people like to have both laces and straps because, during

**Clockwise:
Time Criterium
road shoe; Carnac
LeMond road shoe
and two of the vast
Shimano range.**

a race, straps can loosen under pressure. A recommended brand for this type of shoe is Brancali.

Do wear socks. If you don't, you're opening the door to infection and chafing. Tradition calls for white socks, although this 'rule' seems to be bending these days. What *is* important is that they are made of cotton or a cotton–synthetic material. Don't wear 100%-synthetic socks because your feet will sweat more, especially in the summer.

Gloves and Shoe-covers

Don't believe that in cold weather racing mitts (gloves with the ends of the fingers cut off) will protect your hands from the elements — they won't. The material is too thin to keep you warm and your fingers will be totally exposed. Racing mitts are a warm or dry-weather item of clothing only.

In really cold weather (less than 5°C/41°F), shoe-covers and thick gloves made from a wet-suit material are a must. These are arguably two of the most important items to get because it is from the hands and feet that the body loses most of its heat. When hands and feet become numb, a cyclist more or less loses the four points of balance. With numb hands it becomes hard to hold the handlebars (and to eat), to change gears and to brake. With numb feet, your pedalling efficiency is seriously impaired. And gloves also help to protect you against hand burns or grazing.

Cycling shops should stock heavy-duty cold-weather gloves and shoe-covers. But if they are hard to come by, you could try a windsurfing shop where the gloves are the same and shoe-covers only need a hole cut in their sole for the cleat.

Clockwise from top:
Netti overshoes;
Netti arm-warmers;
Pearl Izumi leather
mitts; Pearl Izumi
winter gloves.

11 Bicycle
Maintenance

The bicycle needs as much care and maintenance as the athlete does. This is simply because no matter how strong and fit you are, you won't get anywhere without a sound working bike.

Maintenance of your bicycle should not be last-minute and sporadic. You should put time aside to clean and check your bicycle regularly for any required repairs. And you should double-check it again before a race.

Cleaning

No matter what environment you live in, washing your bicycle is vital. This is especially important if you've been riding in wet weather or near the sea, where salt on the roads can increase corrosion.

To wash a bike properly, you'll need the following:

- bucket of luke-warm water with a little detergent
- bottle of diesel oil
- sponge
- soft brush
- old toothbrush
- tin or bottle of chrome polish
- selection of dry rags

The first step is to take your bike to an open area where there is no risk of the washed-off dirt or the cleaning materials you are using marking anything. It is often handy to put the bike in a bike-stand. If you don't have this, it is not important — just place it against a wall.

To clean the rims, use a sponge or brush with detergent water. The tyres can be cleaned with a soft brush which will also help pull out any small stones or glass and metal splinters from the tread which you may not see.

If the chain is dirty it should be cleaned with a paintbrush dipped in diesel oil. The same can be done for the brakes, gear levers, the derailleur and free-wheel, or rear, cog. Make sure you do this before you start cleaning the frame.

For the frame, a sponge with soapy water is ideal. However, try as much as possible to avoid getting water into the components cleaned with diesel. After washing thoroughly with a hose fitted with a high-pressure nozzle, dry off the entire bicycle with dry rags or towels. Then apply fresh oil to the chain, gears and brakes. Use the oil sparingly, as a little goes a long way.

Chrome polish should be used now and then on the handlebar stem, seat post, brakes, hubs, spokes, rims, cranks, chain-rings and pedals.

Quick Repairs

Nothing beats having a qualified mechanic attend to any repairs. However, there are several maintenance repairs which you can do yourself. This will save money and the inevitable delay that leaving a bike at a cycling shop will lead to.

An important asset for any cyclist is a good set of cycling tools. There is a huge variety to choose from. What you actually get really does depend on your budget and ability to use the tools. A cycling shop should be able to advise you on what to get for a basic tool kit. This could include:

- foot and hand pumps
- allen keys
- spanners
- screwdriver (with normal and Phillips head pieces)
- spoke key
- plastic tyre levers
- rim cement
- chain and crank-removal tools
- adhesive electrical tape
- tape-measure
- penknife
- scissors
- chain lubricant
- spare tubular tyres, or spare tyres and inner tubes
- spare handlebar tape
- spare spokes
- pen marker, pen and note pad to record positional changes or status

TROUBLESHOOTING
CHART

A bicycle is a dynamic extension of your body. Learn to tune into your bike, so that you automatically listen to it and watch it as you cycle along. The better you ride, the more aware you will become of the bike's mechanical condition. All bikes produce a constant melody of whirs, clicks, and soft hisses that form a rhythmic pattern when all is working well. Listen, look, and feel for unusual noises and riding sensations, and try to track down the source immediately. Use this chart as a rough guide to getting to the root of a problem.

Symptom	Likely Cause	Solution
Knocking or jittering when brakes applied	• Brakes out of adjustment	• Centre brakes and/or adjust brake block toe-in
	• Forks loose in head tube	• Tighten head set
	• Bulge in rim or rim out of true	• True wheel or take rim to a bike shop for repair
	• Brake mounting bolts loose	• Tighten bolts
Brakes do not work effectively	• Brake cables are sticking/stretched/damaged	• Clean/adjust/regrease/replace cables
	• Brake blocks worn down	• Replace blocks
	• Brake blocks/rim greasy, wet or dirty	• Clean blocks and rim
	• Brakes out of adjustment	• Centre brakes
	• Brake levers are binding	• Adjust brake levers
Brakes squeak or squeal when applied	• Brake blocks/rim dirty or wet	• Clean blocks and rim
	• Brake blocks worn down	• Replace blocks
	• Brake block toe-in incorrect	• Correct block toe-in
	• Brake arms loose	• Tighten mounting blocks
Frequent punctures	• Tyre pressure too low	• Correct tyre pressure
	• Spoke protruding into rim	• File down spoke
	• Tyre not checked after previous puncture	• Remove sharp object embedded in tyre
	• Tyre tread/casing worn	• Replace tyre
	• Inner tube old or faulty	• Replace inner tube
	• Tyre unsuited to rim	• Replace with correct tyre
Inaccurate steering	• Head set loose or binding	• Adjust/tighten head set
	• Front forks bent	• Take bike to a bike shop for frame realignment
	• Wheels not aligned	• Check tracking and align wheels

Symptom	Likely Cause	Solution
Wheel wobbles	• Hub cones loose • Wheel out of true • Head set binding	• Adjust hub bearings • True wheel • Adjust head set
Clicking noises when pedalling	• Loose bottom bracket spindle/bearings • Loose pedal axle/bearings • Stiff chain-link • Loose crank set • Bent bottom bracket/pedal axle	• Adjust bottom bracket • Adjust bearing/axle nut • Lubricate chain • Tighten crank bolts • Replace axle
Grinding noises when pedalling	• Bottom bracket bearings too tight • Pedal bearings too tight • Chain hitting derailleurs • Derailleur pulleys dirty/binding	• Adjust bearings • Adjust bearings • Adjust chain line • Clean and lubricate pulleys
Chain jumps off free-wheel sprocket or chain-ring	• Chain-ring loose • Chain-ring out of true • Rear or front derailleur side-to side travel out of adjustment • Chain-ring teeth bent or broken	• Tighten mounting bolts • True if possible or replace • Adjust derailleur travel • Repair or replace chain-ring/set
Chain slips	• Chain worn/stretched • Stiff link in chain • Chain-ring or free-wheel sprocket teeth excessively worn/chipped • Chain/chain-ring free-wheel not compatible	• Replace chain • Lubricate or replace link • Replace chain-ring and sprockets and chain • Seek advice at a bike shop
Gear shifts faulty	• Front or rear derailleur not adjusted properly • Derailleur cables sticking/stretched/damaged • Indexed shifting not adjusted properly	• Adjust derailleurs • Lubricate/tighten/replace cables • Adjust indexing
Free-wheel does not free-wheel	• Pawls are jammed	• Lubricate. If problem persists, replace free-wheel

197

Maintenance

■ Chains, Brake Blocks and Brake Cables

Check these for possible replacement. They all wear out some time or another. It is better to change them before they do — it could happen, leaving you stranded miles away from home!

    The naked eye can verify if brake blocks and cables need replacing. However, it's harder to see if you need a new chain. A handy method is to try and lift the chain off the big chain-ring with two fingers. If three or four chain-links can be raised, then there is too much slack and you should replace the chain. If the cluster is old or worn, it is good practice to replace it as well because new and old equipment don't usually run well together.

■ Hubs

Each year you should dismantle the hubs — or get someone to do it if you can't — and have them cleaned and given a new dose of grease.

■ Handlebar Stems and Seat Posts

Do the same for the handlebar stem and seat post. These two items are easy to take out and only need an allen key to do it. However, before you remove them, make sure you know the position they were in beforehand. A good tip is to lightly mark the stem or post at the point where it goes into the tubing or frame. Make sure you keep these two parts well greased, or you will have the awful task of trying to separate components welded with rust.

■ Cranks and Head Sets

Cranks should be re-tightened and head sets checked for any movement or corrosion. Check the head set for movement by applying the front brake and rocking the bike gently back and forth. If it's loose, you'll hear a clunking noise.

■ Wheels and Spokes

It is important that your wheels are regularly serviced. Major wheel maintenance is a highly specialised job which takes years of experience — you may prefer to have a professional look after customised wheels, but there are checks and repairs you can do at home.

    First check to see that the wheels are 'true' — that is, that they don't wobble when spun. This should be done before and after any race or when you have replaced an old or broken spoke.

Loose spokes can cause wheels to wobble, so check the tension of the spokes, especially in the rear wheel. You'll need a special spoke key for this. It connects with the nipple of the spoke at the rim.

Many riders get confused about which spokes need tightening and in what direction they should be turned. Basically, when the rim wobbles to the right you must loosen the right spokes and tighten the left ones at the troubled area of the rim until the run is true. To tighten a spoke, the key should be turned anti-clockwise and vice versa. When a rim is raised up or bent, it can be corrected by tightening the left and right spokes in the affected area. When the rim is flattened slightly, loosen the spokes on both sides of the flattened area. A good way of preventing spokes from coming loose is to apply a small drop of rim cement or silicon solution on top of each spoke nipple.

◼ Tyres

Check them before and after every ride if possible. Look closely at the tread and remove any splinters or specks of material that might have lodged there. If you find something, deflate the tyre and pick it out delicately with a sharp object like a penknife. Be careful not to 'dig-in' when extracting an object as this may not only push the foreign object further into the tyre, but it might cause the very puncture you are trying to avoid!

Also, if you can't avoid cycling over a patch of broken glass or debris, a way of minimising the chance of anything piercing the tyre is to lightly place a palm (with gloves on, of course!) on the tyre while cycling. Be very careful when doing this. Don't let your fingers bend around the rim and get caught in the spokes. Similarly, don't put too much pressure on the tyre as it may suddenly brake you.

Changing Tyres and Tubes

One of the most important maintenance jobs is changing old tyres or putting new tyres on old rims.

If you have brand-new rims, it's important to clean them first with petrol. Then they'll need three or four base coverings of rim cement before the tyre can be fitted. These layers should be thin, but evenly spread, with the first layer taking 24 hours to dry and the others 10 hours each.

The physical task of putting a brand-new tyre on a rim is not easy. It depends on which type of tyre you are riding: high-pressures are easier to change than singles.

Singles

Before fitting singles, stretch the tyre first. This can be done by placing one foot with your weight behind it on one side, pulling the other side up firmly towards your chin. Make sure that you don't pull too hard, otherwise you'll tear the base tape, causing a weak spot in the new tyre. Do this several times at different points of the tyre.

With this done, it's time to put another layer of cement on the rim. This layer only needs five or ten minutes of drying time before you can start pulling the tyre over and on to the rim. When putting the tyre on, make sure it's slightly inflated and begin by putting the valve area of the tyre on to the rim first.

Place the rim on a clean surface (to avoid grit getting into the cement) and slip the rest of the tyre on. Do this by stretching it further with a pushing action away from you, and manipulating it up on to the rim. To get the last portion on you may need to place the rim against a wall so that the wheel is horizontal to the ground, and then slip it on with your thumb.

A safer way of changing tyres is to put the new tyre on the wheel *without* rim cement; then pump it up to race pressure (100 to 120 psi) and glue it on afterwards.

With the tyre on, roll the wheel as if to check it is true. This time look at the tyre and check that it is evenly positioned on the rim. The cement should still be soft enough for any realignment of the tyre to be easily made. Once you are sure the tyre is on correctly, pump it up and leave it to dry. A recommended drying time is half a day.

There's a strong chance of puncturing during a training ride. To be prepared for this, it's imperative that you have at least one spare tyre and a pump with you on every occasion. For long rides of up to four to six hours, it is advisable to carry two spares.

Tyre levers are very handy in taking off singles which have been stuck on firmly. They can make all the difference in peeling the tyre away from the rim, especially in cold and wet weather.

If you need to change a tyre while training, simply put on a spare tyre without a new spread of cement. This is only a temporary measure to get you home as there will still be the risk of it rolling off. You should always deflate that spare upon returning home, take it off and give the rim a new dose of cement before putting the spare back on again. And don't forget to replace the spare tyre!

High-pressures

With high-pressures, you're spared the sticky difficulties of cement work because the entire inner tube is removed and replaced when punctured. To do this effectively, you should always have a set of plastic tyre levers to help prise the tyre off the rim and expose the inner tube for extraction.

After taking the inner tube out and placing the new one in the tyre, put the valve through the rim hole. Then, using the plastic levers again and working around the rim, slip the tyre and inner tube on to the rim. As you do this, be careful not to pinch the new inner tube between the tyre levers and the rim.

Always carry at least two spare tubes and a high-pressure tyre — it will come in handy if your tyre has a cut in it (a new tube wouldn't last long in a damaged tyre).

Taking care of your bicycle also includes storage at home and packing when travelling.

Storage

When at home, it is recommended that a special location is found for storing all cycling equipment. A garage or basement is an ideal area for this. This helps you to know where everything is and avoids the risk of dirtying the house. It also helps you to maintain a rational perspective on the other priorities in your life which might be impaired by the sometimes omnipresent influence of cycling! By keeping your cycling equipment locked away in a separate area you are reminding yourself and others that cycling is not the only important element in your life.

Once you have located a storage area, it's important to organise it properly. We all have varying and limited space, but be efficient with the space you have.

Try and include a work area in your space. You'll need it when attending to repairs and positional alterations. You could place a work bench in this area and hang tools on the wall. Also, save room for a bike work stool; these are available in most cycling shops. If there isn't enough room under the work bench, you might want a cupboard or drawer for storing loose odds and ends and smaller spare parts like pedals, handlebars, etc.

After you've done that, identify the best place to put your bicycle/s and larger spare equipment. A great space-saver is to hang your bicycle by the front or rear wheel on hooks on a beam or wall. You can do the same for spare wheels and tyres, although try to find a dark area for high-quality tyres — they're like wine and will mature and improve with age in 'cellar-like' conditions!

Packing

When you're travelling, packing a bicycle calls for great care. No matter where you go, or how, there's always the risk of damage. So always insure your bicycle. You can also take several precautions to minimise the odds of harm.

Some people travel on aeroplanes with their bicycle unpacked. They believe this will stop baggage-handlers from throwing it around recklessly, as sometimes happens with bike bags. However, airlines (and other transport services) don't always accept unpacked bicycles. (Another disadvantage of flying with your bike is that some airlines — particularly in the United States — charge for bikes to go on planes.)

If you decide to pack your bicycle, you'll find a good range of cycling bags at most cycling shops. These, however, are expensive and can themselves become damaged. Many people nowadays use cardboard bicycle boxes. These are the boxes bicycles are delivered in — you could ask your local bicycle retailer for one. The advantage of this form of packaging is that if it's damaged, you can easily repair it with packing tape, or get another free box.

When packing a bicycle for the first time, ask an experienced traveller to show you how. Each person has their own little tricks. Here are some recommended steps:

- take off wheels and deflate tyres (for air travel). Remove quick-release axles to maximise space in the bag;

- undo pedals and remove;

- remove handlebars and stem from bicycle for more efficient packing (if you don't remove them, handlebars take up a lot of room, even when turned inwards);

- insert a front axle or small supporting beam between front forks to prevent them being bent en route;

- place cranks parallel to frame and secure position by tying/strapping the chain section near the rear derailleur to the frame;

- wrap frame, rear derailleur, cranks, chain-rings and rear wheel block in protective material like bubbled plastic, foam or a towel;

- place frame in bag upside-down;

- for added security (not everyone does this), insert a sheet of cardboard on either side of the frame;

- slip one wheel on each side of the frame. With the rear wheel, make sure the freewheel, or block, is facing inwards and not rubbing against the frame;

- if possible, place a towel, sheet or thin protective covering over the side of the frame and wheels facing the bag opening;

- zip up the bag and make sure it is well marked with your name and address. It also helps to write *FRAGILE* on it as well!

It's a common tactic to include extra items like foot pumps, spare tyres and light tools in a bike bag. Clothes and shoes can also be added, though they should be put in protective plastic bags to avoid collecting grease marks. Extra packing can provide extra support and protection for the frame, but be realistic with what you can fit in.

Important
Contacts

The following numbers and addresses can be useful for further information. For numbers and contacts of more national bodies and any affiliated cycling associations or comittees, contact the Union Cycliste Internationale or your national association. (Numbers in brackets are country and regional codes in that order.)

International

Union Cycliste Internationale
37 Route de Chavannes
CH–1007 Lausanne
Switzerland
Tel: (41-21) 6260080
Fax: (41-21) 6260088

National

■ Australia
Australian Cyling Federation
68 Broadway
Sydney
NSW 2007
Tel: (61-2) 2818688
Fax: (61-2) 2814236

■ Belgium
Royale Ligue Vélocipédique Belge
49 Avenue du Globe
1190 Brussels
Tel: (32-2) 3491931
Fax: (32-2) 3431256

■ Canada
Association Cycliste Canadienne
1600 Promenade James Naismith Drive
Gloucester
Ontario K1B 5N4
Tel: (1-613) 7485629
Fax: (1-613) 7485692

■ Great Britain
British Cycling Federation
36 Rockingham Road
Kettering
Northants NN16 8HG
Tel: (44-536) 412211
Fax: (44-536) 412142

Ireland

Federation of Irish Cyclists
619 North Circular Road
Dublin 1
Tel: (353-1) 8551522
Fax: (353-1) 8551771

Italy

Federazione Ciclistica Italiana
Stadio Olimpico-Curva Nord
Cancello L-Porta 91
00194 Rome
Tel: (39-6) 36857813
Fax: (39-6) 36857175

Netherlands

Koninklijke Nederlandsche
Wielren Unie
Postbus 136
Polanerbaan 15
3447 GN Woerden
Tel: (31-3480) 11544
Fax: (31-3480) 11437

New Zealand

New Zealand Cycling Association
McHughs Road RD2
Kaiapoi
Tel: (64-3) 3126421
Fax: (64-3) 3126304

Norway

Norges Cyckleforbund
Hauger Skolevei 1
1351 Rud-Oslo 1
Tel: (47-67) 154703
Fax: (47-67) 154903

Oman

Oman Cycling Association
PO Box 6990
Ruwi
Tel: (968) 799647
Fax: (968) 705779

Russia

Union Cycliste de la Russie
119270 Quai Loujnetscaya 8
Moscow
Tel: (7-095) 2011672
Fax: (7-095) 2480814

South Africa

South Africa Cycling Federation
PO Box 4843
Cape Town 8000
Tel: (27-21) 5571212
Fax: (27-21) 5573155

Spain

Federación Española de Ciclismo
Ferraz 16-5
28008 Madrid
Tel: (34-1) 5420421
Fax: (34-1) 5420341

Switzerland

Comité National du Cyclisme
Industriestrasse 47
Case Postale
8152 Glattbrugg
Tel: (41-1) 8101030
Fax: (41-1) 8101180

United States

United States Cycling Federation
1750 East Boulder Street
Colorado Springs
Colorado 80909
Tel: (1-719) 5784581
Fax: (1-719) 5784628

Glossary

bidon: French word for the drink bottle used by cyclists; it is attached to a metal cage on the bicycle frame.

breaks: Formations of cyclists who have attacked and formed their own group and are racing ahead of the main bunch.

commissaire: French; the title is used in cycling to designate the judge. Every cycling event has a head commissaire who is supported by a team.

criterium: An inner-city/town bicycle race. The field races over laps of up to 1.5 kilometres (1 mile) ridden for approximately 1 hour. These races are normally very fast and the courses include many corners.

derailleur: A device which allows the chain to move from one cog to another, or from one front chain-ring to another.

derny: A pedal-activated motorcycle which is used on the track of a velodrome. The derny driver rides in front of cyclists at a higher speed than they would normally pedal at to help them warm up and then to increase their speeds.

domestique: French word used to describe a team rider whose sole duty is to help a designated team leader win a race.

drops: The lower section of the handlebars.

echelon: A formation of riders in single, double or triple-file across the road; cyclists take their turn at the front of the group and at various intervals to form a windbreak for those behind them. The formation depends on the strength and direction of the prevailing winds.

free-wheel: The rear cluster of gears. The number of gears vary, but usually ranges between five and eight.

gruppo: Italian word used in cycling to mean the set of gear componentry on a bicycle.

handler: A back-up person to help someone racing at an event.

head sets: The combining unit between the head stem and adjoining section of the bicycle frame.

maglia rosa: 'Pink jersey' in Italian; it denotes the overall race leader.

maillot amarillo: The yellow jersey of the Tour of Spain worn by the overall race leader.

maillot arc en ciel: French for 'rainbow jersey', it signifies the world champion.

maillot jaune: 'Yellow jersey' in French. This is the overall race leader's jersey in the world's biggest cycling event — the Tour de France.

peloton: French word which collectively describes the field, or main bunch, in a cycle race.

points competition: A competition within every stage race where points are awarded to riders on their placings in stage finishes — and sometimes at

205

intermediate sprints during a stage. The final winner is the rider with the most points.

randonnée: French term for a cycling event where cyclists ride over a set course, but at their own speeds. At selected intervals or checkpoints the riders have a card stamped by officials to verify they have completed that part of the course.

roll-out factor: The distance travelled per pedal revolution according to the gear ratio used.

sitting-on: A commonly used tactic where one cyclist will ride very closely behind another. This move allows the cyclist behind to take advantage of the other's slipstream, and therefore to expend less energy. (However, a rider who *sits* on is one who refuses to take a turn at the front.)

stand-ups or **track stands**: A tactic used by track sprinters where they come to a standstill in the preliminary laps of a match race. The move, where they stop and hold their balance without putting their feet on the ground, is designed to either force the other rider into taking the front position or line of action or to intimidate him or her psychologically.

to make a jump: To step up on the pedals, out of the saddle, to accelerate.

velo: French word for bike.

Bibliography

Australian Cycling Federation Coaching Manual: Level 2, Australian Cycling Federation, Adelaide, 1989.

Cycle Racing, Frank Westell and Ken Evans, Springfield Books, Huddersfield, 1991.

Dictionnaire International du Cyclisme 1993, Claude Sudres, Editions Ronald Hirle, Strasbourg.

1988 Tour de France, Phil Liggett, Harrap, London.

Six Days, Roger de Maertelaere, Uitgeverij Worldstrips, Ghent, 1991.

The Foreign Legion: Breaking the Barriers of European Cycling, Rupert Guinness, Springfield Books, Huddersfield, 1993.

Velo 1994, Harry van den Bremt and Rene Jacobs, Editions Velo, Oudegem.

Velo Records, Harry van den Bremt, Rene Jacobs, Hector Mahau and Rene Pirotte, Editions Velo, Oudegem, 1992.

Appendix

List of Categories
of Doping Substances and Methods

Adopted by the UCI Management Committee on 18 August 1994 on the proposal of the
Antidoping Commission and with the agreement of the UCI Medical Commission
Entry into effect — 1 November 1994

I. Categories of Doping Substances

A. Stimulants
B. Narcotics
C. Anabolic agents:
1. Androgenic anabolising steroids
2. Non-steroidal anabolic agents
D. Peptide hormones and analogues

II. Methods of Doping

A. Blood doping
B. Pharmacological, chemical or physical manipulation

III. Classes of Substances Subject to Certain Restrictions

A. Alcohol
B. Marijuana
C. Local anaesthetics
D. Corticosteroids

IV. Substances Referred to in Article 90(2) of the UCI Antidoping Examination Regulations

A. Caffeine if the urine concentration exceeds 12 micrograms per millilitre in a measurement accepted by the Antidoping Commission which shall decide case-by-case in the light of all the facts.
B. Narcotic analgesics.
C. Ephedrines such as ephedrine proper, cathina (norpseudoephedrine), methylephedrine, phenylpropanolamine, and pseudoephedrine.

V. Substances Prohibited at Out-of-competition Tests

A. Anabolic agents
B. Peptidic hormones
C. Masking agents
D. The following stimulants:
   amineptine
   amphetamine
   amphetaminil
   benzphetamine
   cocaine
   dimethylamphetamine
   ethylamphetamine
   fenetylline
   fenproporex
   forfenorex
   mesocarb
   methoxyphenamine
   methylamphetamine
   methylphenidate
   morazone
   pemoline
   phendimetrazine
   phenmetrazine
   pipradol
   pyrovalerone
E. Compounds chemically or pharmacologically related to the products mentioned under A to D above.
F. Products designated by the UCI Management Committee the names of which shall be published in the Information bulletin.

Notes:
1) This list is based on that of the International Olympic Committee but is not wholly identical thereto. Beta-blockers and diuretics are not considered doping agents with respect to cycling and are not tested for.
2) It is recalled that under the Antidoping Examination Regulations, all products, regardless of denomination containing even minor amounts of the above-mentioned substances are prohibited.

Examples and Explanations

I. Categories of Doping Substances

A. STIMULANTS
such as
amfepramone
amphetaminil
amineptine
amiphenazole
amphetamine
benzphetamine
caffeine*
cathine (norpseudoephedrine)**
chlorphentermine
clobenzorex
clorprenaline
cocaine
cropropamide (constituent of 'Micorene')
crothetamide (constituent of 'Micorene')
dimetamphetamine
ephedrine**
etaphedrine
ethamivan
ethylamphetamine
fencamfamine
fenetylline
fenproporex
furfenorex
mefenorex
mesocarb
methamphetamine
methoxyphenamine
methylephedrine**
methylphenidate
morazone
nikethamide

pemoline
pentetrazol
phendimetrazine
phenmetrazine
phentermine
phenylpropanolamine***
pipadrol
prolintane
propylhexedrine
psuedoephedrine***
pyrovalerone
strychnine (nux vomica)
and related substances

* For caffeine, a sample shall be deemed positive if the concentration in the urine exceeds 12 micrograms/ml.
** For ephedrine, cathine (norpseudoephedrine) and methylephedrine, a sample shall be deemed positive if the concentration in the urine exceeds 5 micrograms/ml.
*** For pseudoephedrine and phenylpropanolamine, a sample shall be deemed positive if the concentration in the urine exceeds 10 micrograms/ml.

Beta 2 agonists
Choosing medication for the treatment of asthma and respiratory difficulties has posed many problems. A few years ago, ephedrine and related substances were often prescribed. However, these substances are forbidden because they belong to the category of 'sympathomimetic amines' and are therefore regarded as stimulants.
Nevertheless, the use of aerosols containing the following 2 agonists only is permitted (how they are used may be determined by the rider):
salbutamol
terbutaline

B. NARCOTIC ANALGESICS
such as
alphaprodine
anileridine
buprenorphine
codeine*
dextromoramide
dextropropoxyphene
diamorphine (heroin)
dihydrocodeine*
dipipanone
ethoheptazine
ethylmorphine
levorphanol
methadone
morphine**

208

nalbuphine
pentazocine
pethidine
phenazocine
trimeperidine
and related substances

Note:
Codeine,* dihydrocodeine, pholcodeine and dextromethorphan
may be used as anti-tussives for medical treatment.
** For morphine (for example, as a metabolite of codeine),
a sample shall be deemed positive if the concentration in the
urine exceeds 1 microgramme/ml.

C. ANABOLIC AGENTS

1 Androgenic anabolic steroids
such as
bolasterone
boldenone
clostebol
dehydrochlormethyl testosterone
fluoxymesterone
mesterolone
methenolone
methandienone
methyltestosterone
nandrolone
norethandrolone
oxandrolone
oxymesterone
oxymetholone
stanozolol
testosterone*
and related substances

* For testosterone, a sample shall be deemed positive if, as a
result of the administration of testosterone or any other
manipulation, the urine testosterone/epitestosterone (T/E)
ratio is increased to more than 6, unless it can be proved that
this ratio is due to a physiological or pathological condition.

Consequently, the Antidoping Commission
recommends that a medical examination,
endocrine tests and longitudinal studies be
carried out to determine whether testosterone
or any other endogenous steroid has been
administered.

With a view to facilitating this evaluation,
UCI-accredited laboratories are requested to
inform the Antidoping Commission of the
results of each case in accordance with the
following criteria:
  A. negative, if the T/E ratio is lower than
     6 or equals 6

  B. positive, if the T/E ratio is above 6
Where point B is concerned, other checks
should be carried out before considering the
result as negative or positive. The tests may
include, amongst other things:
  - a retrospective analysis of previous
    results,
  - endocrinological checks,
  - spot checks spread over a period of
    several months.

2 Non-steroidal anabolic agents
such as:
zeranol
clenbuterol

D. PEPTIDE HORMONES AND ANALOGUES

Chorionic Gonadotrophin (HCG—Human Chorionic Gonadotrophin):
It is well known that the administration of
human chorionic gonadotrophin and other
related compounds leads to an increase in the
production of natural androgenic steroids and
is considered equivalent to the exogenous
administration of testosterone.

The maximum value authorized is 20 ImU/ml
with a specific density of 1.020 g/ml. Two methods
using radio-immunoassays are requested.

Corticotrophin (ACTH):
Corticotrophin has been misused to increase
the levels of endogenous corticosteroids in
the blood, particularly to obtain the mood-
elevating effect of corticosteroids. The
administration of corticotrophin is regarded as
equivalent to the oral, intramuscular or
intravenous administration of corticosteroids.
(See section III.C)

Growth Hormone (HGH Somatotrophin):
The use of growth hormone in sport is
regarded as amoral and dangerous by reason
of its various side-effects such as allergic
reactions, diabetogenic effects, and
acromegaly when administered in large doses.

All release agents of the above-mentioned
substances are also prohibited.

Erythropoietine (EPO)—A glycoproteinic
hormone produced in the human kidney
which regulates, apparently by retroaction,
the rate of synthesis of erythrocytes.

II. Methods of Doping

A. BLOOD DOPING
Blood transfusion is the intravenous administration of red blood corpuscles or blood compounds containing red corpuscles. These products may be obtained from blood extracted either from the same individual (auto-transfusion) or from different individuals (hetero-transfusion). The most common indication for the transfusion of red blood corpuscles in current traditional medicine is a large blood loss or severe anaemia.

Blood doping is the administration of blood or related substances containing red blood corpuscles to an athlete for reasons other than legitimate medical treatment.

This procedure may be preceded by the taking of blood from the athlete, who then goes on with his training in a state of blood insufficiency.

These practices contravene the ethics both of sportsmanship and of the medical profession. Moreover, there are risks associated with the transfusion of blood or blood substances. These risks include the development of allergic reactions (skin rashes, fevers, etc.) and also acute haemolytic reactions with kidney damage if an incorrect blood type is used, as well as delayed reactions to transfusion such as fever or jaundice, the transmission of infectious diseases (viral hepatitis and AIDS), the overloading of the circulatory system and metabolic shock. Consequently the practice of blood doping in sport is prohibited.

B. PHARMACOLOGICAL, CHEMICAL OR PHYSICAL MANIPULATION
The use of substances and methods which alter the integrity and validity of urine samples used in drug tests is prohibited. Amongst the methods prohibited let us cite catheterisation, the substitution and/or alteration of urine and the inhibition of renal excretion, particularly through probenecide and related compounds, and the administration of epitestosterone. If the concentration of epitestosterone is above 150 mg/ml, laboratories are requested to

notify the authorities concerned. The Antidoping Commission recommends in this event that additional checks be carried out.

III. Categories of Substances Subject to Certain Restrictions

A. ALCOHOL
Alcohol is not prohibited. However, the alcohol level in the breath or blood may be tested on request.

B. MARIJUANA
Marijuana is not prohibited. However, checks may be carried out at the request of a federation.

C. LOCAL ANAESTHETICS
The injection of local anaesthetics is permitted on the following conditions to be determined by the rider:
a) that procaine, xylocaine, carbocaine, etc. be used — but not cocaine.
b) that only local and intra-articular injections be given.
c) only when their use is justified on medical grounds.

D. CORTICOSTEROIDS
Natural or synthetic corticosteroids are used above all as anti-inflammatory substances which also relieve pain. They also have an effect on the concentrations of natural corticosteroids in circulation in the body. They bring about a certain euphoria and have such side-effects that their medical use, except for topical application, necessitates medical checking.

The use of corticosteroids is prohibited, except when used for topical application (auricular, ophthalmological or dermatological), inhalations (asthma and allergic rhinitis) and local or intra-articular injections. Such forms of utilisation are to be determined by the rider.

Index

Permissions

The publishers would like to thank the following organisations for permission to reproduce material:

Perigee Books, New York, for the Sizing Chart, Metric Conversion Chart and Variations on Frame Geometry on pages 4 and 7 and the Gear Ratios Chart on pages 20–21 from *Greg LeMond's Complete Book of Bicycling*, © Greg LeMond and Kent Gordis, 1987.

Dorling Kindersley Ltd., London, for the Troubleshooting Chart on pages 196 and 197, from *Richards' Bicycle Repair Manual* by Richard Ballantine and Richard Grant, Dorling Kindersley Ltd., 1992.

Union Cycliste Internationale, Lausanne, for the List of Categories of Doping Substances and Methods on pages 207–10.

Picture Credits

All photographs are by Graham Watson (© Graham Watson), except those listed below, which were supplied and reproduced with the permission of the following people or organisations:

News Ltd: page v.

Bicycle Institute of New South Wales: pages 1, 68, 99.

Robbi Newman: pages 10, 12–13, 14–15, 16, 17, 19, 22, 25, 26, 42–43, 56–7, 66–7, 71, 85, 126, 188, 190, 191, 192, 193.

Sport: The Library: Col Stewart: page 54–5; Jeff Crow: page 59; Steve Casimiro: page 101; Al Messserschmidt: page 125; Clifford White: page 167. Phil Latz, *Bicycling Australia*: page 70.

The publishers would also like to thank the following people and organisations for their help:

Racheal Appleton; Matt Haran; Tony Sattler; Stanmore Cycles; Cranks Bike Shop, Roseville; Manly Cycle Centre.